# Essential Guides for
# EARLY CAREER
# TEACHERS

# Workload
## Taking Ownership of your Teaching

# Essential Guides for Early Career Teachers

The *Essential Guides for Early Career Teachers* provide accessible, carefully researched, quick-reads for early career teachers, covering the key topics you will encounter during your training year and first two years of teaching. They complement and are fully in line with the new *Early Career Framework* and are intended to assist ongoing professional development by bringing together current information and thinking on each area in one convenient place. The texts are edited by Emma Hollis, Executive Director of NASBTT (the National Association of School-Based Teacher Trainers), who brings a wealth of experience, expertise and knowledge to the series.

Why not explore the other books in this series?

*Essential Guides for Early Career Teachers: Assessment*
Alys Finch
Paperback ISBN: 978-1-912508-93-8

*Essential Guides for Early Career Teachers: Mental Well-being and Self Care*
Sally Price
Paperback ISBN: 978-1-912508-97-6

*Essential Guides for Early Career Teachers: Special Educational Needs and Disability*
Anita Devi
Paperback ISBN: 978-1-913063-29-0

*Essential Guides for Early Career Teachers: Understanding and Developing Positive Behaviour in Schools*
Patrick Garton
Paperback ISBN: 978-1-913453-09-1

*Essential Guides for Early Career Teachers: Workload – Taking Ownership of your Teaching*
Julie Greer
Paperback ISBN: 978-1-913453-41-1

Our titles are also available in a range of electronic formats. To order, or for details of our bulk discounts, please go to our website www.criticalpublishing.com or contact our distributor, NBN International, 10 Thornbury Road, Plymouth PL6 7PP, telephone 01752 202301 or email orders@nbninternational.com.

# Essential Guides for
# EARLY CAREER
# TEACHERS

## Workload
### Taking Ownership
### of your Teaching

NASBTT

Julie Greer
Series editor: Emma Hollis

First published in 2020 by Critical Publishing Ltd

British Library Cataloguing in Publication Data
A CIP record for this book is available from the British Library

ISBN: 978-1-913453-41-1

This book is also available in the following e-book formats:

MOBI ISBN: 978-1-913453-42-8
EPUB ISBN: 978-1-913453-43-5
Adobe e-book ISBN: 978-1-913453-44-2

Cartoon illustrations by Élisabeth Eudes-Pascal represented by GCI
Cover and text design by Out of House Limited
Project management by Newgen Publishing UK
Printed and bound in Great Britain by 4edge, Essex

Critical Publishing
3 Connaught Road
St Albans
AL3 5RX

www.criticalpublishing.com

Paper from responsible sources

# Contents

# Meet the series editor

### Emma Hollis

I am Executive Director of NASBTT (the National Association of School-Based Teacher Trainers) and my absolute passion is teacher education. After gaining a first-class degree in psychology, I trained as a primary teacher, and soon became head of Initial Teacher Training for a SCITT provider. I am dedicated to ensuring teachers are given access to high-quality professional development at the early stages of and throughout their careers.

# Meet the author

### Julie Greer

I have been a primary headteacher for half my life, making the most of my own early career experiences in inner London to form my passion for education and my determination to make a difference for all members of a school community. I try to achieve this through a combination of aspiration, offsetting disadvantage and seeking fairness. I have a particular interest in special educational needs and disabilities, including the social, emotional and mental health needs of children. I work closely with the Anna Freud Centre, supporting the work of the Mental Health and Wellbeing in Schools programme. I am a Visiting Fellow at the University of Southampton and a Founding Fellow of the Chartered College of Teaching. I have been a member of the National Executive of the Universities' Council for the Education of Teachers (UCET) and of the Schools Reference Group. Through this I have advocated for positive developments in teacher education.

# Foreword

As a passionate advocate of high-quality teacher education and continuing professional development, it has always been a source of frustration for me that beyond the Initial Teacher Training year, access to high-quality, structured ongoing professional development has always been something of a lottery for teachers. Access and support has been patchy, with some schools and local authorities offering fantastic opportunities for teachers throughout their careers while in other locations CPD has been given lip service at best and, at worst, is non-existent.

This series was conceived of to attempt to close some of those gaps and to offer accessible professional learning to busy teachers in the early stages of their careers. It was therefore a moment of genuine pleasure when proposals for an entitlement for all early career teachers to receive a package of support, guidance and education landed on my desk. There is now a genuine opportunity for school communities to work together to offer the very best early career development for our most precious of resources – the teachers in our schools.

The aim of this series is to distil some of the key topics which occupy the thoughts of early career teachers into digestible, informative texts which will promote discussion, contemplation and reflection and will spark further exploration into practice. In each edition, you will find a series of practical suggestions for how you can put the 'big idea' in each chapter into practice: now, next week and in the long term. By offering opportunities to bring the learning into the classroom in very concrete ways, we hope to help embed many of the principles we share into your day-to-day teaching.

Any brief look at the research on teacher retention will quickly reveal that significant numbers of teachers leave the profession within the first five years. The reasons behind this are complex, but workload is frequently cited as a key driver for teachers choosing to leave. An obvious solution might be seen to be to reduce workload and retain more teachers. However, the concept of workload is a complicated one which does not stand up to such a simplistic view. Teachers' views of what constitutes 'manageable' and 'excessive' workloads are nuanced and cannot be easily defined. In this title, Julie expertly explores these nuances, leading you through an exploration of what acceptable workload means to you in your particular context and offering practical, actionable ways to achieve a sense of balance in your career.

I hope you enjoy exploring this book as much as I have enjoyed editing it.

*Emma Hollis*
Executive Director, NASBTT

# Acknowledgements

It hasn't been without irony that I have been writing a book on workload during the response to the global coronavirus pandemic, during which school leaders have had to undertake a huge number of additional tasks and make major shifts in the way we risk assess, lead our teams and make our school communities safe places to continue teaching and learning. The staff and governors at Cherbourg Primary have risen to this challenge and our parents, carers and children have responded. They are all such a wonderful team to work with and make my own workload achievable (mostly) and a pleasure (always). As staff, we have been on our own journey to find a professionally acceptable workload and their ideas and feedback have helped to challenge my own previously set notions and informed parts of this book. They remind me that this should always be an evolving process and an ongoing part of our professional development. Thank you.

To Paul and my family for their endless support and encouragement and for occasionally reminding me to step away from my laptop and to my daughters, who inspire me with their own enthusiasm and idealism for what you can achieve in teaching, thank you.

I appreciate Enitharmon Press for giving permission to use U A Fanthorpe's poem *Sisyphus* in the introduction. Thank you to Catherine and Madie for their time spent reading.

I am grateful to the National Executive of the Universities' Council for the Education of Teachers (UCET) who supported my early efforts to respond to the Department for Education's School Workload Reduction Toolkit, alongside Caroline Daly from the UCL Institute of Education, so that the discourse on a professionally acceptable workload could begin from the outset of a teacher's training. When Caroline and I gave the closing afternoon keynote speech on teacher workload at the UCET conference in November 2019, the hall was unusually packed – not because it was us, but because the subject matter is recognised as so vital to improving teacher retention and recruitment over the next few years.

Thank you to Emma Hollis and the National Association of School-Based Teacher Trainers (NASBTT), and Julia Morris of Critical Publishing, for producing a series that is making a difference to those new to the profession. I hope this book will be a further contribution to teachers having agency and balance in their workload and enable mentors and teacher educators to support the start of long and fulfilling careers for the next generation of teachers.

# Introduction

## *Sisyphus* by U A Fanthorpe

'The struggle itself towards the heights is enough to fill a man's heart. One must imagine Sisyphus happy.'

Camus, *The Myth of Sisyphus*

Apparently I rank as one
Of the more noteworthy sights down here.
As to that, I can't judge, having
No time to spare for tourists.

My preoccupations are this stone
And this hill. I have to push
The one up the other.

A trivial task for a team, an engine,
A pair of horses. The interest lies
Not in the difficulty of the doing,
But the difficulty for the doer. I accept this
As my vocation: to do what I cannot do.
The stone and I are

Close. I know its every wart, its ribby ridges,
Its snags, its lips. And the stone knows me,
Cheek, chin and shoulders, elbow, groin, shin, toe,
Muscle, bone, cartilage and muddied skinprint,
My surfaces, my angles and my levers.

The hill I know by heart too,
Have studied incline, foothold, grain,
With watchmaker's patience.

Concentration is mutual. The hill
Is hostile to the stone and me.
The stone resents me and the hill.

But I am the mover. I cannot afford
To spend energy on emotion. I push
The stone up the hill. At the top

*It falls, and I pursue it,*
*To heave it up again. Time not spent*
*On doing this is squandered time.*

*The gods must have had a reason*
*For setting me this task. I have forgotten it,*
*And I do not care.*

(Fanthorpe, 2013)

Workload is a heavy word, not just in its connotations, but in the physical sound of it too. And teacher workload is indeed a weighty issue for schools and individuals in the twenty-first century. Like Sisyphus interminably pushing the boulder uphill, the interest in this handbook lies '*not in the difficulty of the doing, but the difficulty for the doer*'. As a teacher you need to work hard throughout your career, just as you would in many other professions. And teachers do want to work hard. Most teachers come into the profession to make a difference and they recognise early on the importance of hard work in achieving this goal (Nias, 1989); yet too often something goes awry. The latest Teaching and Learning International Survey (TALIS) report shows that teacher hours are higher for primary and lower secondary teachers in England than in most other Organisation for Economic Co-operation and Development (OECD) countries (Jerrim and Sams, 2019). However, the number of hours which teachers work is only one aspect and doesn't capture the global nature of concerns relating to teacher workload. Klassen et al (2013) surveyed four countries across the world to conclude that teacher stress was mostly derived from pupil behaviour and workload. A quick internet search will show that many countries have dedicated webpages addressing concerns related to teacher workload.

In their advice to school leaders, mentors and appropriate bodies on supporting early career teachers, the Department for Education (DfE) notes:

*Workload is one of the most commonly cited drivers for teachers leaving the profession, and 33% of teachers leave the profession within the first five years. The Teacher Workload Survey 2016 identified that teachers with less than six years' experience report higher average working hours per week than more experienced colleagues.*

(DfE, 2019, p 3)

This drop-out not only has an impact on the supply of good teachers and consequences for children's learning and outcomes, but it also brings into question the economic waste of training teachers only to lose them from the profession so quickly. To badly misquote Oscar Wilde, it would suggest that losing nearly one-sixth of teachers in the first year after qualification may be regarded as misfortune; to lose one-third after five years looks like carelessness (Office for National Statistics, 2019)!

The most recent analysis of the Schools Workforce Survey (Office for National Statistics, 2019) also highlights that 5.4 per cent of teachers decreased their working hours, either by moving from full- to part-time working or by remaining part-time but decreasing their weekly hours. While this data includes teachers across the profession, these changes in working patterns resulted in the approximate equivalent of 3200 full-time equivalent (FTE) qualified teachers leaving the profession between 2018 and 2019. The impact on early career teachers of more experienced teachers leaving the profession warrants further exploration, but your relationships with your colleagues and the culture within your school can make a huge difference to how you feel about your teacher identity, your resilience, your workload and consequently whether you feel you can manage to have a career in balance with your whole life.

The use of the term *professionally acceptable workload* throughout the book came about as a response to the Department for Education's *Workload Reduction Toolkit* and associated papers in 2018. It was important to find a way to capture work as an essential and positive means of carrying out the role of teaching effectively, while inferring the individual and collective responsibilities in achieving this. It was also vital to locate the word firmly within a professional status, from which an informed debate could take place on what was acceptable and what was not.

The *Workload Reduction Toolkit* is designed for schools to address the issues surrounding time spent on unnecessary tasks and additional processes and encourages school leaders to work with whole staff teams to tackle this. It is not a one-off obligation, but an ongoing conversation. Ofsted inspections of schools in England now focus on workload, placing the emphasis on school leaders and whether they have been effective in making reductions of unnecessary tasks (Ofsted, 2019). Ofsted also states clearly that it will '*not create unnecessary workload for teachers through its recommendations*' (p 13), which is an honourable intention, but less easy to enforce. It is perhaps similar to saying '*Just bring yourselves!*' to a dinner party. Most people would interpret this as meaning that it is still better to bring something, even if it is something small. In other words, while the host might genuinely intend guests to just bring themselves, the hosts also realise that that is unlikely to happen.

A Department for Education report summarises school-based short research projects on the uses of the workload toolkit. The Education Development Trust trained, supported and co-ordinated the teachers' research. The report found that '*teacher designed interventions significantly reduced teacher time conducting the targeted tasks, i.e. approaches to marking and feedback, lesson planning, managing pupil data, internal communications, and lesson observation and monitoring*' (Churches, 2020, p 4). Although reasonable, an emphasis on reduction of hours is also reductionist of the wider issues relating to teacher stress. Within a performative culture, it may be too easy for school leaders to pursue means of reducing hours spent working and increasing staff measures of well-being and still leave teachers feeling overwhelmed and uninvolved in these decisions.

How you feel about workload is a personal perception and involves many other factors. The COVID-19 global pandemic has had a huge impact on teachers as key workers during the lockdown of spring and summer 2020. Teachers had to adapt and adopt new practices, both within school and to support online learning. It also required an increased range of non-teaching tasks, such as making phone or email contact with children whose presence was not visible online or in school. This brought a host of new and different challenges and stress for teachers, but it also brought a general reduction of teaching hours for many teachers. However, as they worked to juggle the invasion of out-of-school needs (for example, childcare, concern for vulnerable family and friends, shopping shortages and medical needs) combined with the new challenges of teaching and working remotely, anecdotally, many teachers still raised legitimate concerns about their workload and how to manage it. This highlights the relationship between anxiety and perceptions of workload and the very personal relationship each teacher has with their response to workload.

Your perception of your role, status, obligations and responsibilities can affect whether you see work tasks as positive or negative; essential or onerous. Your impressions of how others perceive you can also shape your reactions and responses to challenge, affecting your well-being and resilience. Taking a look at how you perceive workload and how this perception shapes your reactions and response to challenge will be a theme throughout the book. Other themes in the book are the importance of agency – you having a say in the decisions which affect you; emotional capital – the language used and its power on how you feel about your role; and balance – finding effective ways to have a fulfilling career, alongside other aspects of life.

You learn well when you are playful with ideas and the book has been written using rich imagery and diverse references, to enable you to play with the concept of a professionally acceptable workload. This book will challenge the way you think about being a teacher. While predominantly addressing your professional self, the tasks and reflections will also require you to look more personally at times.

Schools need to be committed to reducing workload and supporting the well-being of their communities, staff and children alike, as both these in turn can impact improved outcomes for children. In schools where the leadership and the school culture are supportive of this ambition, change will happen. This book is for you and the changes you can make to ensure you have a happy and fulfilling teaching career.

# References

Churches, R (2020) *Supporting Teachers Through the School Workload Reduction Toolkit.* Education Development Trust. London: Department for Education. [online] Available at: https://assets.publishing.service.gov.uk/government/uploads/system/uploads/attachment_data/file/899756/Supporting_teachers_through_the_school_workload_reduction_toolkit_March_2020.pdf (accessed 30 July 2020).

Department for Education (DfE) (2019) *Reducing Workload: Supporting Teachers in the Early Stages of Their Career. Advice for School Leaders, Induction Tutors, Mentors and Appropriate Bodies.* [online] Available at: https://assets.publishing.service.gov.uk/government/uploads/system/uploads/attachment_data/file/786178/Advice_for_ECTs_update.pdf (accessed 29 July 2020).

Fanthorpe, U A (2013) *U A Fanthorpe: Selected Poems.* London: Enitharmon Press.

Jerrim, J and Sams, S (2019) *The Teaching and Learning International Survey (TALIS) 2018.* Research report, Department for Education. [online] Available at: https://assets.publishing.service.gov.uk/government/uploads/system/uploads/attachment_data/file/809737/TALIS_2018_research.pdf (accessed 29 July 2020).

Klassen, R, Wilson, E, Siu, A F Y, Hannok, W, Wong, M, Wongsri, N, Sonthisap, P, Pibulchol, C, Buranachaitavee, Y and Jansem, A (2013) Preservice Teachers' Work Stress, Self-efficacy, and Occupational Commitment in Four Countries. *European Journal of Psychology of Education,* 28: 1289–1309. [online] Available at: https://link.springer.com/article/10.1007/s10212-012-0166-x (accessed 29 July 2020).

Nias, J (1989) *Primary Teachers Talking: A Study of Teaching and Work.* London: Routledge.

Office for National Statistics (2020) School Workforce in England: Reporting Year 2019. [online] Available at: https//explore-education-statistics.service.gov.uk/find-statistics/school-workforce-in-england#releaseHeadlines-dataBlock-charts (accessed 29 July 2020).

Office of Standards in Education, Children's Services and Skills (Ofsted) (2019) *School Inspection Handbook.* London: Ofsted Publications. Available at: https://assets.publishing.service.gov.uk/government/uploads/system/uploads/attachment_data/file/843108/School_inspection_handbook_-_section_5.pdf (accessed 29 July 2020).

# Endorsements

*This is an extremely timely and helpful book which will be of real interest to new teachers and those who support them. Especially given the challenging times we live in.*

James Noble Rogers, Executive Director UCET

*This authoritative guide to tackling teacher workload is both timely and welcome. Julie Greer writes from the perspective of having chalked up considerable experience and expertise as both teacher and headteacher. Those of us who have been fortunate enough to hear her speak on this topic will recognise immediately her passion as well as her deep seated commitment to actually empowering class teachers to think anew about how best to manage the complexities of their work. Rarely, if ever, has anyone pulled together such a range of practical and reflective strategies designed to truly secure a teacher's work-life balance.*

*Investing your own valuable time in this metaphor-rich and highly readable book will, undoubtedly, pay dividends.*

Kim Francis,
NASBTT Trustee and NASBTT Awards 2019 Outstanding Contribution to ITT

*This book is an invaluable source of guidance and support for early career teachers, their mentors and managers. It provides useful practical strategies alongside a sound academic base. The wealth of experience of the author comes through and will provide both reassurance and inspiration for teachers at the start of their careers. We must do more to support school staff to ensure that their mental health and well-being is prioritised. This book will contribute to conversations that keep teacher well-being high on the agenda in relation to their workload from the very beginning of their careers.*

Jaime Smith
Director of the Mental Health and Wellbeing in Schools Programme
Anna Freud National Centre For Children and Families

*Workload remains a huge issue for many teachers, and while much needs to be done to tackle this at a system level, for a new teacher it is also crucial to develop and understand strategies for managing workload. This book provides an excellent primer - and manages to be both informative and, perhaps unexpectedly, also an entertaining read!*

*With a focus on how we can ensure teachers have a 'professionally acceptable workload', the book covers a range of topics and things to consider, from how we perceive our role as teachers to managing work creep. Reflective and practical tasks throughout help ensure ideas are embedded and adopted in practice. Perhaps most importantly, the key themes that come up throughout are agency and balance - both critically important for all teachers, not just those starting out their career.*

Cat Scutt
Director of Education and Research, Chartered College of Teaching

*Every new teacher worries about managing workload! This timely and essential guide really helps. It's much more than a guide; it's like having a daily mentoring dialogue sharing the insight and considered reflections of an experienced practitioner. This book is chock full of ideas, examples and practical tasks – wrapped in memorable metaphors (goldmining, packing saddles, Buckaroos) to engage early career teachers. It will strengthen the confidence and professional self-identity of the teacher as well as the pragmatic balancing between work and life required to succeed.*

Margaret Mulholland
Inclusion Specialist and Honorary Norham Fellow of
Oxford University's Department of Education

# Chapter 1  Saddlebags or saddled with baggage?

## What? (The big idea) ◀◀◀

### The importance of good packing!

Whether you are familiar with a horse or not, most people can conjure up an image of *Buckaroo*, the children's game in which the mule pays you back for overloading her by kicking out and sending all the gold-mining equipment across the room. This is a good metaphor for what can happen when you misjudge the fine balance needed to manage your role as a teacher. Managing a teaching workload is like packing a road horse for a long and often arduous journey. You need to think carefully about what you will need today, tomorrow and next week. You have to think about how what you pack for today might affect what you will need in a couple of months' time. You need to make sure you have got the basics covered, but also plan for some events that might be less foreseeable. You may have to pack what other people have told you to include and you may have to leave off something that you really wanted to have with you, but don't have room for. Sometimes you may need to throw something off so that you can offer a ride to a fellow traveller in need.

If ever there was a time in your teaching career when you are likely to overload, you would think it would be at the start of your journey, when you're still working out what is important, what can be prioritised and what is a good investment of time to save you time later. But sadly, this is not the case. There is no magic solution that you suddenly learn two years in, which means you never suffer the stress of overwork and overload again. Too many teachers find it challenging and difficult to saddle up their horses for those long journeys.

Adding to the imagery of professional teacher workload as being like a well-packed horse, CuChulaine O'Reilly of the Long Riders Guild writes, in Chapter 30 of the *Horse Travel Handbook*:

> It is essential that the panniers be as closely balanced as possible. Even the difference of a few too many ounces heavier on one side may pull the saddle off side. This in turn creates pressure, which causes saddle sores that can quickly ruin a trip.
>
> (O'Reilly, 2015, p 44)

That all sounds pretty painful and best avoided! Whether you see your panniers as tasks to be done, responsibilities to bear, or relationships to make and maintain, the list of items to pack can quickly become overwhelming.

The question of balance is important and features in later chapters. For now, focus on what is in those saddle bags. How often do you insist on carrying additional baggage and how often are extra bags given to you to add to your load?

This chapter should help you to shape your thinking in a way that makes loading those saddle bags a positive experience for you, rather than you feeling saddled with bags of guilt, stress, pressure and a low sense of worth. Instead of being exhausted by the amount of baggage, which in turn impacts on those around you, you can take time to pack with care, leaving you with energy, purpose and clarity focused on the most important thing you do – enabling children to learn and thrive. A well-saddled horse is the equivalent of a professionally acceptable workload.

# So what?

Adjusting your perception of your role, and finding ways to take ownership of the decisions you make about that role and the tasks you undertake, can make a big difference to how professionally competent you feel and your confidence to undertake it. A feeling of having no control can often contribute to increased stress and anxiety. You will recognise this as a theme throughout the book.

Depending on what you read and who you talk to, there are many ways to break down the aspects of the teaching role. The *Early Career Framework* (DfE, 2019a) refers to five overall sections, which are set out in eight standards in line with the

Department for Education *Teachers' Standards*. This is streamlined with the Core Content Framework for Initial Teacher Training (DfE, 2019b). Alongside these eight standards there is also Part 2 of the *Teachers' Standards* (DfE, 2011), which refers to personal and professional conduct. Managing teacher workload advice from the Department for Education classifies areas for focus in slightly different ways. Much research on workload balance will attest that there is no 'right way' to define where this balance comes from, as it is different for each individual, but in looking at task-driven load it is helpful to have a broad definition from which to start.

There are seven key areas set out below that you need to consider if you are to reach a professionally acceptable workload:

1. assessment;

2. communication;

3. meeting needs;

4. performance management;

5. planning;

6. resourcing;

7. training and development.

In making the list, it would have been easy to argue, for example, that performance management and training and development thread across areas of planning and meeting needs, but in relation to workload, there are specific tasks for each area that need consideration, so they have their own category. You may find it remiss that delivery of lessons is not included; but while teaching lessons can be exhilarating, exhausting, pleasurable and stressful in sometimes equal measures, it could be argued that if you manage the work related to these areas above, then delivery of a lesson doesn't create its own workload. However, if the list doesn't sing to you, you may prefer to use the *Teachers' Standards,* or create your own classification. All of these tasks are designed to help you, so please make them your own.

## Reflective task (part 1) ◀◀◀

Using the following table, make a list of as many of the tasks or aspects related to each category as you can think of and consider whether you find them doable or difficult. You can apply your own definition, but 'difficult' is probably those tasks which you don't want to start, that you feel take you longer than they should and which don't give you much positive feedback. A better word may be 'onerous'.

There may be many challenging tasks that take a long time to complete that end up in your doable list, however, so it is not a simple list of 'easy' versus 'hard' tasks.

It may be easier to do this with a colleague or friend. It is not a definitive list and there is no right answer. You can change the columns to your preferred categories. It is not designed as a tick-off task, but something you may want to return to over time. It is the method, or process, of sorting and decision making that is useful in this exercise.

|  | Doable | Difficult |
| --- | --- | --- |
| Assessment |  |  |
| Communication |  |  |
| Meeting needs |  |  |
| Performance management |  |  |
| Planning |  |  |
| Resources |  |  |
| Training and development |  |  |

## Example using the reflective task ◀◀◀

Once you've completed the grid, it might look a bit like the example below.

|  | Doable | Difficult |
| --- | --- | --- |
| Training and development | • Annual online training modules for health and safety.<br><br>• Inset days where we get involved.<br><br>• Reading social media, highlighted short articles related to education and learning.<br><br>• Professional conversations with colleagues.<br><br>• Action research in the classroom.<br><br>• Staff meetings.<br><br>• Observing colleagues. | • Writing up training log.<br><br>• Inset days where we are instructed.<br><br>• Longer reading, such as recommended books or academic articles.<br><br>• Writing up action research<br><br>• Staff meetings when I'm thinking about something else, or when I've had a bad day.<br><br>• Online surveys from the Senior Management Team (SMT). |

## Reflective task (part 2) ◄◄◄

Take a look across both sections and undertake the following activities, in order. You will need three highlighters and a pencil. Remember to be honest with yourself: this is not for anyone else other than you. Don't lose your list when you've finished as there is a further part to this task later in the chapter.

1. Highlight any tasks that you find *pleasurable* while doing them.

2. In a different colour, highlight any that you find *pleasurable* when you reflect on the difference the task has made to the children's learning, or to you professionally.

3. In a third colour, highlight those aspects that have a *positive impact* for children (there will be overlap with your previous highlights, so work out a way to manage this, so it is clear for you).

4. Then, consider how you might prioritise the tasks or roles in relation to their impact on the teaching and learning in your class. Jot a number by the side of each; 1 being the top priority, 2 the second, etc.

5. Now, put an asterisk next to any that at this stage in your career you only do because you are told to do them by your Senior Management Team.

6. Lastly, look at those areas that you ranked last. Are any of them highlighted? If they are ranked last and have no highlight, what is their purpose? Why are they on your list? Where do the aspects you coded for SMT come in your list?

Too often, teachers undertake tasks because the culture of the school is set and *'things have always been done that way here'*. The task above is designed to test what you would 'pack' onto your horse and what you might choose to leave behind. The importance of the activity is to enable you to take ownership of the decisions which are in your control and to have a better understanding of the purpose of the tasks you are required to do. By understanding the purpose, you may find a route to better motivate yourself for the task.

What about those tasks you have identified as lacking purpose and having little value?

• Do you have the power to stop doing this particular task, or tasks?

• Do you feel empowered to discuss this with your mentor, or a colleague?

• Can you think of a better way to undertake an unpleasant task that has an important purpose?

One of the aims of this book is to support you to take ownership of your workload and recognise the correlation between what you do and the impact it has for children. There are many aspects of a teacher's job that are imposed by those who hold more power. The way this is done differs greatly from school to school, depending on the school culture, or habitus, but there are very few school management structures that would welcome a teacher in their early career questioning the way things are done by being negative and subversive. Most staff will at some point moan about what they have to do and the lack of ownership they feel they have. However, falling into negative and unconstructive collusion with those who 'don't want to' is not the purpose of these chapters. Taking ownership over the decisions that you can make and finding agency to help shape change in the workplace is a more positive and effective use of your energy.

Thinking carefully about intent and impact will give you a useful vocabulary to open a discussion about the need for implementing tasks that give you cause for concern in relation to your workload. Like most people, senior managers are not great at feeling criticised or undermined, but that should never mean there is no room for critique, accountability and change. It just means you have to be smart about how you go about it! Senior managers would usually prefer a staff member to approach them with a solution rather than a problem. Asking for their advice while proposing a solution works well, for example. Asking to trial a different way of doing something and then presenting the evidence is also a positive way forward.

## Case study ◀◀◀

A newly qualified teacher (NQT) in Year 2 who works part time was concerned about finding time for managing planning, preparation and assessment (PPA), alongside effective handover in the short PPA time available to her. In an email to her head she wrote:

> I know when we spoke yesterday, you were helpful in suggesting some ways to help me organise my time, but I was still worrying about this in the night and hoped you might like my idea. I am very much an early morning person, rather than a late night worker and as my NQT time is first thing on a Tuesday, I was wondering if every other week or so I could work at home and come in for 10.30. This would mean that I could start my tasks early in the morning and work through, when I am focused and uninterrupted. I would come in on alternate weeks to meet my mentor and would of course come in early if my NQT time changed. If I could do this, I think I would feel more on top of things and then be better focused in my PPA with the rest of the team.

After a few months, the teacher found she preferred to work in school in her non-contact time, but having some control over her decisions helped her to reduce her anxiety.

## Time after time

Unlike most professions, a teacher's role has a flexible, temporal narrative, but what does this really mean? A teacher's role can feel quite fixed, particularly for those in their early career and for those who perceive that they have too little control over the timetables and routines. However, although daily routines may not be that flexible in themselves, teachers constantly switch between time scales and time labels in the abstract, in order to meet the different demands of the role. For example, you may be talking to a child in a French lesson, realise that the child has a gap in his understanding of the future tense, make a mental note to build that into next week's lesson as a refresher for all pupils, but monitor this over the half term for this particular child.

Teachers learn to do this in quite a skilled way very quickly in their career, partly because the structure and rhythms of the academic year are already familiar from experiencing school as a pupil. This often means, however, that teachers don't get a chance to reflect on the purpose of these structures and how they might be improved to better support a learning community, including the teachers.

Looking at the following list, can you add any other time structures that you use regularly or occasionally?:

» daily;

» weekly;

» half-termly;

» termly;

» holidays;

» academic yearly.

Within each of these structures there are additional time labels. These are words which hold a constant meaning but which also denote regular patterns of time, such as lesson, break, assembly, golden time, lunch. For example, you may not know the content of the weekly assembly in advance, but you will know roughly how long it will take.

There is also a great deal of repetition in teacher tasks, which you might interpret as monotony, or you might consider safe and doable. The tedium of repetitive tasks is discussed further in Chapter 5.

## Reflective task (part 3) ◀◀◀

Once you have thought about what tasks and roles you need to do, you need to think about how to allocate the tasks appropriately and effectively into these timescales to achieve a professionally acceptable workload.

Think about the tasks you have identified in your doable/difficult table and how they fit within your timelines. If it is helpful, you can photocopy your list, or rewrite it out and then cut it up and put the tasks into the time zones in which you feel they belong. You may need duplicates, as some will fit into several time structures. For example, completing your online health and safety training may be an annual event, whereas curriculum planning may be a daily, weekly, half-termly, termly and annual job.

This task will help you 'pack your horse', or in other words, support you to organise your packing for different parts of your school year. There is no benefit to getting stressed about doing your online health and safety training in September if it is not due until June. However, if you can make a note to factor it into your scheduling for the second half of the summer term, then you won't have the stress of reminders from SMT in July.

1. Put each of your tasks into the middle column, in the row(s) that is the best match.

| Category, eg assessment | | |
|---|---|---|
| Time structure | Task or aspect of role | Priority (abc) |
| Daily | eg marking | |
| Weekly | | |
| Half-termly | | |
| Termly | eg pupil progress meeting | |
| Academic annually | | |
| Non-pupil facing time | | |

2. Highlight the tasks that can be done during teaching time in one colour.

3. In a second colour, highlight the tasks that you would prefer to do in your non-contact time within school (eg with other colleagues).

4. Highlight in a third colour the tasks that you would prefer to do at home at a time of your choosing. Note that a full-time teacher has 1265 hours of directed time across 195 working days; time when the head can direct your work, or work availability. This equates to about 32.5 hours each week. If you are not able to negotiate some flexibility in where you carry out some of your directed tasks, such as planning and assessment, then you do have a say in where you carry out the remaining hours you work in a week. Use this colour to create your ideal scenario of home tasks.

5. Next, prioritise the order in which you think you should undertake the tasks within each row, *a* as the highest priority, *b* the second highest etc. For example, within a day, which of these tasks you have identified would be the one you think you should do first: a) marking alongside the child; b) reflecting on which children need catch-up input before the next lesson; c) writing questions to prompt further thinking in five books?

- Are the areas you alphabetised in priority order similar to the areas you numbered as having the greatest impact on teaching and learning?

- How can you explain any discrepancies?

- Is there a correlation between tasks you feel you have to do first, or last, and those that you had identified as being tasks that SMT ask you to undertake (those with an asterisk)?

- Is there a pattern between those tasks you find pleasurable and the order in which you have chosen to do them?

There are still no right or wrong answers, but in reflecting on your priorities and task allocation in this way, you stop doing jobs 'just because they're always done this way' and you develop better strategies to engage intellectually with your professional role.

One period of time that needs particular consideration in relation to workload is holidays. As a teacher, your terms and conditions state that you have 13 weeks' holiday (DfE, 2019c). The *Oxford English Dictionary* defines holidays as '*an extended period of leisure and recreation, especially one spent away from home or in travelling*' and probably so does your subconscious! This might mean that whenever you feel you should work during the 13 weeks you perhaps feel cheated, or noble (or both!). If you choose to work, it may be helpful to think about those 13 weeks as non-pupil facing and from there you can decide which days and weeks you take as leave and which you use effectively to work, by catching up, planning ahead, researching, reading, developing and thriving professionally, regardless of whether you are in the school building or not. Making grown-up decisions about when to work and when not to during a period when you do have autonomy can be very empowering.

It may be helpful to mark this out on a calendar of non-pupil facing days, but don't be too hard on yourself if you change your mind on a sunny day you had marked as a working day.

# Now what? ◀ ◀ ◀

## Never put off 'til tomorrow...

Research by Laybourn et al (2019) used qualitative methods to examine the relationship between stress, emotion and teacher procrastination:

> *Contemporary definitions propose that procrastination entails a self-regulatory failure (Sirois and Pychyl, 2013; Anderson, 2016) in terms of voluntarily and needlessly delaying an intended action (Wohl et al., 2010) despite knowing or expecting to be worse off for the delay (Steel, 2007).*
>
> (Laybourn et al, 2019, p 2)

Straight away this definition might make you feel guilty. But the study shows that this can be destructive behaviour, which makes those who engage in it feel bad about themselves, during and after the doing of it. Because there is an element of self-destruction within this action, whether knowingly or unknowingly, it is an important element to raise, and bad habits can also be hard to break.

It is not the doing of other things while you have 'important things' to do that is the problem per se: it is allowing yourself to take on a different task in order *to avoid* the first task that is the problem. Not everyone is disciplined and driven, with the skills to focus and prepare everything without a deadline looming (or missed!). Learning a little more about how to understand procrastination, its destructive potential and how to embrace a little diversion without negative impact might be useful for you.

Although the number of teachers involved in the study was small, the interview data is rich and the findings important. The study recognised that teachers need to have high levels of self-regulation to manage their frequent independence.

From an initial study set of 27 male and female teachers in Germany, nine teachers self-reported that they never needlessly delayed tasks, or found their own approach to task management to be negative or stressful. The remaining 16 took part in the research and identified that they demonstrated procrastination behaviour in the following areas:

» correcting students' work;

» administration and organisation;

» preparing lessons;

» evaluating students on their general work and performance.

The main reason they gave for their behaviour was task aversiveness; that is, they found the task they were avoiding to be '*boring, uninteresting or effortful*'. Other reasons included:

» resistance to extrinsic pressure – a task that they have been told to do by others;

» hedonism – the preference for activities that were perceived to give more immediate pleasure, even though this was often dulled by guilt or stress;

» self-doubt about competence – not a view necessarily shared by others;

» fear of failure – including where expectations of what could be achieved were high;

» poor working conditions – nowhere quiet to work, or poor access to technology.

The research found that teachers often took work home, where procrastination behaviour was higher. This doesn't mean that working from home will always result in diversionary behaviour, but it is important to recognise that it is easier to 'legitimise' distractions in the home. '*I'll just pop the washing on*'; '*Oh, we've run out of milk*', or '*I've been meaning to clean that bathroom for weeks!*' If you need to get some milk and you have reports to write, make a pact with yourself to write five, then take 20 minutes off to nip to the shop and reward yourself with a cup of tea before you get back to work. Take ownership of your wants and structure them around your needs, rather than the other way around.

Interestingly, the study into teacher procrastination found that teachers were more likely to show avoidant and aversive behaviour when the tasks lacked meaning and where tasks were imposed, leaving the teachers with no sense of ownership. Among the teachers interviewed, the researchers found that while procrastination resulted in a range of negative emotions for teachers, such as anger, guilt and disappointment, overall the teachers only felt this behaviour to be moderately stressful. It is unclear whether these same teachers reported higher levels of stress in relation to the tasks they had avoided, however. It may be that the pleasurable aspect of avoidant behaviour can be harnessed and used more effectively as intrinsic reward for tasks undertaken, giving yourself permission to enjoy other activities for a period, reducing the guilt, and ensuring ten minutes having a cup of tea in the sunshine, or an hour talking with a friend, is not at the expense of the original task that needs doing. A better knowledge of your own purpose and priorities should help you plan in this way.

Teaching is a profession in which staff are generally required to have high levels of self-regulation and intrinsic motivation, but in the UK and many other countries this is offset by systems of regulation and performance management that are reliant on quantitative measures and extrinsic approval – a sometimes frustrating dichotomy. Chapter 4 explores teacher agency and how you can still take some ownership of the decisions which affect you, even within systems that are often decided by others.

## Practical task for tomorrow: sleeping under the stars

One thing that can be hard to achieve when there are lots of things going round in your head is a good night's sleep and yet it can make all the difference to how you feel about yourself and the rest of the world!

A really good technique that works well for some people might seem counter-intuitive, but is worth a go when work thoughts keep popping into your head. Instead of trying to relax or thinking of gentle or low-stimulus images, such as counting sheep, embrace the frenetic thoughts by focusing intently on one very detailed idea and create a picture in your mind.

For example, imagine yourself getting off your horse, feeling the ground under your feet, which have been pressured by the stirrups for a long time. In your mind's eye, take the reins and feel the leather run across your palm as you tie it to a nearby tree. Seek in your head to smell the tree bark as you get close to it. If you're still awake by this point, don't panic, just carry on the story. Walk the few steps back to your horse and notice what is around you in the clearing. Try to really see it in your mind. Open your pack and take out a blanket, feel its raspy warmth and lay it on the ground. Wrap your coat around you and lay down under the stars.

This technique works best with as much detail as you can manage and it can work night after night with the same narrative. You can choose your own story and images, build in an ice cream treat from a kiosk at the seaside, or warm yourself by a logfire on the beach.

Sleep tight!

## Practical task for next week: what's in your bag? ◀◀◀

The tasks earlier in this chapter are good for planning and organising your professional workload for regular and known tasks, but one of the frustrating things you might find are all the 'extras' that crop up: some of your own making and many more that are imposed. For example, you are all set for the next couple of days and then the Special Educational Needs and Disabilities Co-ordinator (SENDCO) asks you to complete a strengths and difficulties questionnaire for a child in your class who has got a Child and Adolescent Mental Health Service (CAMHS) appointment in two days' time. She apologises but she has only just received it and needs it back tomorrow morning. You've never done one before, you want to get it right, you worry that a lot might rest on where you put your ticks and you don't want to let the child down. Consequently, it takes you a lot longer than it would for an experienced teacher. Suddenly, all the things you were hoping to finish before you went home are still waiting for you.

You've been thinking about how to pack for the long journeys, but what do you need for shorter trips that will help you to get through your working week, leaving room for those extras? Some of the decisions about additional things to do are likely to be as a result of choices you make, for example, when you decided to spend nearly half an hour trying to find a good film clip for your English lesson and ended up watching online clips of animals doing hilarious things. However, much of your work does make a difference to those children you teach.

So for the next week, before you go home each evening from school, stop and unpack your bag. Put back the things that you need, the tasks that you know you have time and motivation to do that evening and the things that are valuable (don't forget your keys and your bank cards).

Don't take the things that you know you won't do, the things that will shout at you all evening from the bag and make you feel guilty. Make a choice about when you are going to do that task. Are you going to come in early the next day to do it? Are you going to take them home tomorrow as you know you have time then? Are you going to stay now for another 20 minutes to get it done before you go home?

Try this all week and see if it has an effect on how you manage your workload.

## Practical task for the long term: a long ride ◀◀◀

The reflective tasks in this chapter are good to keep returning to over the coming months and terms. Building the skills to reflect on your previous reflections (a means of being reflexive) will help you to take an academic approach to your professional skills. See if you can persuade some of your team to do the task with you too, or talk with a colleague about the choices that you made.

Giving yourself permission to reflect on your workload choices and decisions is important, as it would be easy to make this a task that you can put to one side in favour of the seemingly more pressing aspects of your job. But if you can get this right early in your career, your later self will thank you for it.

# What next? ◄ ◄ ◄

## Further thinking

You are back on the trusty horse, towards the end of this chapter, heading off down a sometimes dusty road as a new sunrise dawns. You know where you are headed; you've planned for some rest breaks along the way, with some stop-offs to admire the view too; you know what is in each of your packs; you've prepared your panniers so the things you are likely to need today are in front of the things you may need later in the week; you have your trusty blanket to comfort you and, perhaps most importantly, you love your horse, your horse responds to you and you'd rather be on this road than any other. Yeehah!

## Further reading

*Early Career Framework* – a two-year programme of support and development for teachers after Initial Teacher Training, devised by the Department for Education. Available at: https://assets.publishing.service.gov.uk/government/uploads/system/uploads/attachment_data/file/913646/Early-Career_Framework.pdf (accessed 18 August 2020).

*Early Career Framework Handbook* – a companion to the *Early Career Framework,* published by the Chartered College of Education in June 2020, with Sage Publishers.

*Encyclopaedia of Equestrian Exploration,* Vol 1 – a comprehensive guide for anyone considering long riding. Written by CuChulaine O'Reilly in 2017 and published by the Long Riders' Guild Press in Glasgow, Kentucky.

Teach Thought – a blog article with some useful ideas and advice for teachers. [online] Available at: www.teachthought.com/pedagogy/25-things-successful-teachers-do-differently (accessed 18 August 2020).

# References

Department for Education (DfE) (2011) *Teachers' Standards*. [online] Available at: https://assets.publishing.service.gov.uk/government/uploads/system/uploads/attachment_data/file/665522/Teachers_standard_information.pdf (accessed 14 September 2020).

Department for Education (DfE) (2019a) *Early Career Framework*. [online] Available at: https://assets.publishing.service.gov.uk/government/uploads/system/uploads/attachment_data/file/913646/Early-Career_Framework.pdf (accessed 14 September 2020).

Department for Education (DfE) (2019b) *Core Content Framework for Initial Teacher Training*. [online] Available at: http://assets.publishing.service.gov.uk/government/uploads/system/uploads/attachment_data/file/843676/Initial_teacher_training_core_content_framework.pdf (accessed 14 September 2020).

Department for Education (DfE) (2019c) *School Teachers' Pay and Conditions Document 2019 and Guidance on School Teachers' Pay and Conditions*. [online] Available at: https://assets.publishing.service.gov.uk/government/uploads/system/uploads/attachment_data/file/832634/School_teachers_pay_and_conditions_2019.pdf (accessed 18 August 2020).

Laybourn, S, Frenzel, A C and Fenzl, T (2019) Teacher Procrastination, Emotions, and Stress: A Qualitative Study. *Frontiers in Psychology*. [online] Available at: www.frontiersin.org/articles/10.3389/fpsyg.2019.02325/full (accessed 14 September 2020).

O'Reilly, C (2015) *Horse Travel Handbook*. Glasgow, KY: Long Riders' Guild Press.

# Chapter 2    It's a circus!

# What? (The big idea) ◀◀ ◀

## Showtime or showdown?

Every teacher has their own unique blend of characteristics, skills, preferences and personality. As P T Barnum said (not the real one, but his eponymous character in the 2017 film *The Greatest Showman*): *'No one ever made a difference by being the same as everyone else!'* However, seeing how your personal approach to your professional workload is similar to others can help you manage times of stress, times of leisure and deadlines with better self-regulation, impacting on how you perform as a teacher in your classroom.

In Perryman and Calvert's (2020) research into teacher retention, using data from five years of teacher education graduates from University College London, 69 per cent of teachers identified *'wanting to make a difference'* as a reason for going into teaching. The authors reviewed studies from Australia and Boston, where there were similar findings, including *'contributing to society'* and *'helping others'* among the main arguments for joining the profession. Many teachers are characteristically altruistic, but many also recognise an early desire to progress towards leadership, to thrive intellectually and to develop professionally. All good reasons for becoming a teacher. However, this same research focused on why so many teachers set out with high hopes, alongside a seemingly realistic notion of the workload to come, and yet within a few years had stopped teaching, citing workload as the predominant reason. Keeping teachers teaching, otherwise known as the retention rate, is a challenge for successive governments. Data gathered since 1997 shows that, every year, between a third and two-fifths of teachers leave the state education sector for reasons other than retirement or death. The Department for Education's most recent statistics, within *School Workforce in England: November 2018*, show that a fifth of new teachers leave the state sector within two years and a third within five years (Foster, 2019, p 9). In a separate prior survey of former teachers, by the Department for Education (CooperGibson Research/DfE, 2018), workload was given as the predominant reason for leaving.

You're probably reading this book because you recognise that teacher workload has the potential to be an issue for you and other teachers. It is hopeful to know that you can acquire the skills and strategies needed to keep your professional workload manageable and your motivation to teach high.

In thinking about teaching, stamina and motivation, it may be helpful to consider how, at the start of her career, an aerial artist learns to leap from the trapeze through the air towards a partner while moving at precarious speed. As the months and years go on, the artist doesn't lose those skills, but fine tunes and strengthens the proficiency required. But although the potential is still there, once the performer loses sight of the impact of her skills on the audience, the desire and the motivation to perform lessens and the risks and downsides of the role take on a greater importance. From that great height, the artist no longer sees the smiling faces and excited anticipation of the crowd, but instead feels the pain in the knees and worries that the trust has gone. Keeping focused on your skills and strengths and the difference you can make to pupils will help you to maintain a long and rewarding teaching career.

# So what? ◀◀◀

## Teaching as performance

In this chapter you are encouraged to learn more about how your characteristics as a teacher can affect your approach to your workload. You are asked to consider how the external drive for higher standards can impact on your motivation and your perception of your capacity. In discovering more about your own approach to performance, you can find out ways to thrive in the spotlight, rather than feel judged by the audience!

Many teachers love the performance element of their role: the ability to tell a story; bring a battle to life; draw out empathy with the evacuee; share excitement over a chemical change or the beauty of an equation. This doesn't need to be loud and elaborate. The performance of a teacher can be equally effective when quiet, gentle and knowledgeable: making a difference to the pupil.

Like circuses, studies in teacher characteristics are a little out of vogue, but there is still a great deal to be learned from the wisdom of the past. It can sometimes be too easy to only look to contemporary education research, so go to the archives sometimes if you are looking for inspiration. A paper by Turner and Denny (1969) from a small study in Indiana, the United States in the mid-1960s, noted '*that teachers characterized as warm and spontaneous and teachers characterized as child-centered tend to obtain the greater positive changes in pupil creativity*'. They observed that these changes appeared to be a result of classroom behaviours that involved '*positive reinforcement of pupil responses, through adaptation of activities to pupils, through attention to individuals, and through variation in activities and materials*' (Turner and Denny, 1969, p 270). In other words, what we already know to be good teaching: effective, inclusive, child-centred pedagogy and task design informed by varied assessment of learning and knowledge of the child's needs. The five characteristics on which the researchers focused were:

1. warmth/spontaneity;

2. involvement;

3. educational viewpoint (child-centred versus subject-centred);

4. organisation;

5. stability.

While they were primarily looking for the evidence of that elusive magician, *Creativity*, they found that pupils were less likely to demonstrate divergent thinking with teachers who rated high in organisation, perhaps because these teachers were less confident to model the characteristics of flexibility and sensitivity to problems that were demonstrated in pupils who showed creativity. The authors' starting point had been that teacher characteristics affect classroom behaviours and pupil characteristics; therefore, a teacher whose characteristics were compatible with a creative style was more likely to bring forth creativity from a child.

Forty years later, educationalists know a lot more about creativity, but there is also the counterpoint of performativity with which teachers and pupils need to contend. An explanation of performativity comes later in this chapter but, in relation to education, performativity can be briefly described as a system in which those who teach are judged on the outcomes of teaching alone. The same system then perpetuates itself to measure only what is measurable and loses sight of what also has value for pupils' learning. Burnard and White (2008) looked at both creativity and performativity and compared them in British and Australian education. Like many others, they recognise that:

> creativity is eminently suited to the multiple needs of life in the twenty-first century, which calls for enhanced skills of adaptation, flexibility, initiative and the ability to use knowledge in different ways.
>
> (Burnard and White, 2008, p 668)

Like the earlier research, Burnard and White (2008) note the characteristics within pedagogical practice which were more likely to develop and enhance creativity. These include 'passing more control to students, providing space and time which enable risk-taking and student agency' (p 671). They also remark that providing these opportunities as a teacher, while 'adhering to the performance agenda and its standards of measured achievement' (p 671) is difficult and conflicting.

Performativity has a huge impact on workload and on how you perceive your role. Finding out more about this notion later on in this chapter may help you to better understand the pressures on you – making more sense of your workload and prioritising who your performance is for and for whom you want to perform and make that difference.

## Reflective task ◀◀◀

### Welcome to the circus!

- Consider the roles below and which aspects you recognise in yourself in relation to how you approach your workload. Use the chart at the end of the descriptions to record your impressions.

### The ringmaster

You have some control over your own workload, but you are not the circus owner. You feel a sense of responsibility for how the performance is viewed by others, but this can sometimes make you ask others to do things you wouldn't want to do yourself. You portray a sense of pride over everything that happens and people trust you to be well organised.

## The juggler

You have so many balls in the air! It takes focus and continuous concentration (you can't take your eye off the ball!), but while it is going well, it works fine and everyone is impressed. Of course, when you drop a ball, or someone throws a knife into the mix, then all the objects tumble to the ground, leaving you to pick up the pieces.

## The lion tamer

You like taking risks. You take on tasks that others don't want to do, but this challenge doesn't worry you as you are confident in your skills and being well organised. Sometimes though, you can seek thrills rather than pride in achieving a task. This can result in you making mistakes and not preparing well enough. You can get away with this sometimes, but may have to deal with the consequences of one very angry lion.

## The acrobat

You're a team player. You like giving your best, you are skilled and flexible and you can do your role by yourself, but you work most effectively when you are with your colleagues – supporting them and being supported in equal measure. It is important to be in peak fitness to do the job, but you recognise that you need to have plenty of rest too, so that you can perform to your best when you need to.

## The tightrope walker

You balance your work and your play with fine precision. You're very aware of the precarious nature of your balancing act, but you're good at it. At times, someone puts an extra weight on one end of the pole, which means you can no longer hold the pole in the middle, but instead you have to work out where the tipping point is and readjust. You have to keep in peak fitness, and look after your hands and feet in particular. You rely on others to make sure that your rope is taut and your safety net is ready for the occasions you are trying new heights.

## The fire eater

You leave everything until the last minute, until the momentum has risen to an inescapable crescendo. Your ability to procrastinate is a skill in itself. You see this as part of your preparation though, but you can also get frustrated with yourself, as you know that if you just set to it and shoot the flames into the air, without all the preamble, you could get on and do other things. If truth be told, most of your audience just want you to get on with it too, although the task is certainly more impressive if you have spent a great deal of time making everyone think you are not capable of it before you achieve it with great flare.

## The trapeze artist

Timing is all. You like to work in bursts on tasks that excite you. The rest of the time you are happy waiting for the right moment. You know the importance of trusting your colleagues and for them to have trust in you too. You are pretty good at hanging out though, and you have a great ability for looking really chilled and relaxed one minute and then flying through the air, upside down, the next. Your moments of effort are brilliant, but other performers may feel that you get a lot of attention for the amount of time you are focused. They don't necessarily see all the time you spend preparing when no one is looking.

## The clown

Yes, you make everyone laugh and see yourself as responsible for keeping others happy, but people don't always realise how hard you have to work at this. Making people feel good about themselves is easier for some than others, but it also requires skill and empathy. You work out how far you can go and who needs more careful handling than others. When you get clumsy, people stop laughing and you find that hard. You know that to keep people laughing you need to produce new stunts (although you think that often the old ones are the best) and it is important to keep your resources up to date and working well (what use is a trick flower that doesn't spray water effectively?). When you are feeling on top of your game you are amazing, but at the end of the performance, you have the ability to take off the costume and the make-up and be your own person.

## The magician

It's all smoke and mirrors. You don't want the audience to look too closely or they might see the rabbit already in the hat. You are good at what you do and you practise your skills regularly to keep your hands deft and your equipment working, but your most important attribute is your ability to charm and distract from reality – look over there, not over here. This works well for you and you do get job satisfaction, but you know it is a bit like the candyfloss the audience like to eat. Looks impressive, but no real substance and won't have any long-term nutritional effect. You might be better working at your card tricks, on a smaller scale, and sharing some of the tricks of the trade. This requires skill and performance, but leaves your audience with a real insight and appreciation into how the magic works and may give you much better job satisfaction.

- Can you recognise your own characteristics in any of these descriptions of circus performers?

- Are there aspects of your approach to your professional workload that are not captured here?

- Is there a character that you would rather be? You can learn skills, but can you change your characteristics? Can you be a lion tamer if you are at heart an acrobat?

- Take the one you feel best describes how you approach your professional role. Draw yourself in costume.

- With the characteristics of this performer, do you think you have good enough skills to manage your professional workload? Make a personal plan to address some of the deficits. There is an example to help you. Be playful with the idea, but try to reach a professional purpose in your plan.

| | Do you recognise this description in your own professional performance? | What aspects of the description do you see as helpful in managing your workload? | What aspects of the description do you see as unhelpful in managing your workload? |
|---|---|---|---|
| Ringmaster | | | |
| Juggler | | | |
| Lion tamer | | | |
| Acrobat | | | |
| Tightrope walker | | | |
| Fire eater | | | |
| Trapeze artist | | | |
| Clown | | | |
| Magician | | | |

## Example ◀◀◀

| Performer | Downsides | My short plan to improve |
|-----------|-----------|--------------------------|
| Fire eater | Always worried I might lose my nerve. | Download a meditation app. |
| | Never practise as much as I probably should. | Reward myself each time I practise. |
| | Play a lot of games when I'm not working. | Use downtime more creatively – ask a colleague to mentor me to learn new skills. |
| | Frequently smell of petrol! | |

## Case study ◀◀◀

### The showman

Ajay had always wanted to teach but had been distracted by the bright lights of business after he developed an app while studying for his history degree. He had the skills for marketing his product and made a good income, but he found managing his business and finances quite stressful and felt he was always having to produce more and better to keep up with other new apps coming out. He moved back in with his parents and went to his local university to train to be a teacher.

*It was great to start with. I was a bit more confident and mature than many of the other trainees, because I'd had my own business. I hadn't had much of a chance to spend time in schools beforehand, unlike some of them, but I thought I would be able to pick it up. My placements went well, but it did sometimes feel like my mentor and tutor couldn't see through me, that they thought I was great, but they couldn't see the panic inside me each lesson. Sometimes I would actually be sick at breaktime, but then go back in the class and smile and joke. The children loved my seemingly carefree approach, but I was forever worried that I was entertaining them and not teaching them. I got my first teaching post easily but then everything changed. The head didn't seem to like me at all and my NQT mentor just wanted me to show her evidence on paper of everything that I was doing. Suddenly I was having the opposite experience, feeling like the people with all the power were just out to expose the fraud I already felt, but didn't want to invest in me to make me the good teacher I knew I could be. I couldn't keep up with all the marking, planning and assessments that were constantly being scrutinised and criticised. I got really low. I moved schools for my final NQT term, which was a gamble, but I was failing already. My new school team are great. They worked with me to know what I wanted to develop and recognised where my skills worked well and where I needed to improve. I don't clown about with my class to distract them, but instead use my humour to engage them in learning.*

## Teaching as performative

*In the performative accountability culture of education in the twenty-first century, efficiency is seen as 'a good thing' irrespective of the cost to people – intensification, loss of autonomy, monitoring and appraisal, limited participation in decision making and lack of personal development are not considered. Thus, teaching and learning are determined in accordance with learning outcomes and objectives. The teacher becomes just another learning resource, a facilitator, where teaching is theorised as the application of fixed recipes and the variety of good practice can be suppressed.*

(Perryman and Calvert, 2020, p 6)

Stephen Ball is an influential source on performativity. Describing what is needed to meet the agenda of performativity, he highlights skills of '*presentation and inflation, making the most of ourselves, making a spectacle of ourselves*' (Ball, 2012, p 19). He argues that this leads to feelings of transparency and emptiness for the person under scrutiny and quotes Judith Butler (2004, p 15): '*I am other to myself precisely at the place where I expect to be myself*'. As a new teacher you may recognise yourself within that powerful quote. At precisely the moment you have a sense of pride in achieving your goal to become a teacher, you may feel you haven't found the identity as a teacher you were expecting; instead, you may feel overwhelmed by the burden of being something other than you imagined. Chapter 3 supports you to look at your identity as a teacher in more detail, but this notion of mismatch may be difficult to contemplate. It is important to remember that there are always friends and colleagues who can help.

Burnard and White (2008) present three strands of performativity:

1. performativity as masquerade;

2. performativity as development;

3. performativity as productivity.

The first strand uses an example given by Judith Butler who exposed 'gender' as performative, noting how each performance of gendered expectations conforms to a social construct. In the present day, the notion of gender can be more fluid in our language and our understanding; however, many parents, educators and advertisers are still reinforcing a concept of gender on young children which needs challenging: for example, throwaway comments like *'that's not a boy's colour'* or the design of girls' shoes and sandals not allowing the freedom to run and leap in the way boys' shoes can, even from a young age. You may also have noticed performative parenting, where an adult uses language loudly to announce and pronounce their public ideal of parenting for all those around them to hear: *'Let's go now Taylor, we have to make your vitamin boost smoothie before your Russian juggling tutor arrives'*, leaving the audience of parents in the playground with a mixture of surprise, annoyance and perhaps shame that they haven't organised a Russian juggling tutor or smoothies for their child! Similar mixed feelings can occur within performative teaching.

Burnard and White (2008) also argue that perceptions of teacher performance are influenced by images in films, for example, of what makes a good teacher or a 'bad' teacher. The impact of a teacher being measured as good or bad within their school can affect pay, development opportunities and professional esteem. The standards against which performance is measured have become increasingly reductionist, stifling teachers' creativity. School leaders have a responsibility to challenge their own perceptions of good and bad teachers, recognising when their own judgements are influenced by subjective or biased viewpoints. You have a responsibility to demonstrate the range of your abilities within the classroom, to meet the needs of all your pupils. You may also need to learn which skills and strengths you need to showcase when being observed, or in professional conversations. You can do this and still be true to yourself. This may seem topsy-turvy, in that it should be the managers who are able to deduce and recognise your true strengths, but learning when to offer ethical opposition and professional critique and when to comply or conform can make a big difference to your stress and workload. The magic trick lies in your performance not being an illusion, but a true part of what you are capable of – just not all you are capable of.

The second strand looks at the *doing* as performativity and *done* as performance. They suggest that the emphasis on performativity is therefore in the training of teaching and the performance once a teacher is in school. This doesn't quite capture the notion of continuous professional development for teachers in schools, but perhaps notes that this can be equally constrained by a performative agenda – when was the last time you got to go on a course that wasn't about standards?

Lastly, they look to the French philosopher François Lyotard, restating his notion that *'performativity represents the attitude of valuing the "effective" and the "efficient" in systems where the least "input" produces the greatest "output"'* (Burnard and White, 2008, p 674). As this suggests, there can be very good uses of performativity within an economic system, driving down waste and improving production, but it is when performativity becomes the system that the conflict arises. In applying performativity to all educational sectors, the drive to deliver aspects of learning and teaching that can be measured through quantitative summative test scores, such as SATs, has made it difficult to value and maintain those aspects of learning and teaching which are harder to define. Governments, media and business leaders respond to and repeat the clarion call for higher, longer, faster, rather than leading the change to notice wider, rounder and deeper. Disappointingly, where Ofsted made good attempts to promote a move away from quantitative data in school inspection in September 2019, the notion of 'deep diving' into the impact of children's learning in subject areas quickly sparked a mass of systems to measure deep dives and the phrase now has the potential to send a chill through teaching staff across England.

Writing about the impact of performativity on the higher education sector, Ball (2012, p 19) states:

> We are burdened with the responsibility to perform, and if we do not we are in danger of being seen as irresponsible. Performativity is a moral system that subverts and re-orients us to its ends. It makes us responsible for our performance and for the performance of others.

Overwhelmed by the need to be accountable, many institution and school leaders knowingly, or inadvertently, create policies and procedures which perpetuate a system of performativity – of measurement and judgement. For example, a school has a bullying policy which emphasises the recording of bullying incidents instead of resolving them. Schools do need to record bullying data for national collation, but it would be far better if governors monitored the percentage where the children felt there was resolution, rather than the raw data of number of incidents. This would quickly impact on practice. You can be an agency of change for your generation of teachers, accepting responsibility for making a difference to the pupils in your care, by all means measuring their progress, because it helps you to know what you need to do next to support them, but not allowing yourself to be solely measured by this.

# Now what?

## Hear that drum roll!

Whichever circus star you felt yourself to be most like, you can be sure that each one will also have their periods of doubt and moments of performance nerves. It can be too easy to get caught up in thinking about your own stress, your own troubles, your own views on the unfairness of a system that leaves you exhausted each evening. The reluctant performer standing outside the Big Top inhales the smell of the grease paint, hears the band playing their tune, feels their pulse quicken as the ringmaster announces their arrival and, as the audience thrill in their act, they remember why they do this, day after day.

## Practical task for tomorrow ◀◀◀

### You are the ringmaster in your own classroom

You have found out which performer you recognise in your attitude and approach to workload, but in your own classroom you are the ringmaster, responsible for the performance of your pupils. Having learned a little about your characteristics, what can you see in your pupils? Can you spot the clown and the fire eater? Does your teaching draw out their strengths or do the demands on you mean that you treat them all as trapeze artists, even though many of them are afraid of heights?

It is worth remembering how you feel when you are being asked to 'perform' for others who hold more power than you. In your classroom you hold the power, so as you plan your lesson for tomorrow, add a few columns in which you write appropriate strategies for more democratic teaching. There is nothing wrong with wanting all your children to fly high, but you do need to consider how the task you are designing can help your children to climb the ladder, if they're not already swinging from the trapeze. While it might be another layer of planning initially, it will help you prepare for all your learners and reduce your anxiety in the lesson. Once you have got the hang of this, a few short notes will suffice.

| Which children are likely to need some support in order to fly high in this lesson? | What are likely to be the barriers to their learning or their misconceptions so far? | Ways I will approach or adapt the task for this group or individual. |
|---|---|---|
|  |  |  |

## Practical task for next week ◀◀◀

### Remember your audience

As if you need reminding, your audience are the children, not the adults. If you are someone who came into teaching to make a difference, it is the pupils to whom you make that difference, not the senior leaders or inspectors. You will know you are doing well, because you will develop the skills to see learning taking place and acquire the understanding of the gaps and know what you need to teach next and to whom. You will thrive professionally because you will take pride in demonstrating the learning journeys your pupils are on.

Think about a series of lessons that went well recently. Without producing a data sheet, how could you present these lessons to your senior managers so that they can understand what the children achieved and what you are going to focus on next for groups or individuals within the class? What will you need to show them? What will you need to describe? Can you do all this without creating extra work for the discussion? Will you be brave enough to present the work of the child who still has many gaps? Do you need to talk with a colleague to help you with the next steps for this child first?

## Practical task for the long term ◀◀◀

You could always run away and join a circus, but running away is never a great idea. Developing an ongoing dialogue between yourself and other colleagues, both in the workplace and further afield using online blogs and networks, will result in far better outcomes for you and your pupils. Add to the reflective journal that you may have started in Chapter 1. Make simple notes when you recognise that you have used a characteristic that has been highlighted in the chapter, or one you have noticed yourself, to feel successful in your role. Highlight where you have deliberately invoked a characteristic to overcome a difficulty – for example, if you were able to draw out the acrobat in you for a team meeting, even though you are usually a lone magician. Jot down the name of a colleague from whom you can learn and be clear about what it is you think you could learn from them and then approach them. Most colleagues will be pleased that you have noticed a good quality in them and they may be only too happy to help you in return by giving you a high five or a signal every time they spot you using the skill or attribute you wanted to learn from them. Roll up and roll up your sleeves for the thrill of a lifetime teaching career!

# What next? ◀◀◀

Ask a group of teachers to shout out what they are good at in their role and most will struggle. Ask them where they think they go wrong and you will find it hard to stop them. Teachers all too often see their faults rather than their strengths. This can make it hard to reflect meaningfully on developing your skills and you may find it emotionally draining at times. It is really important to look out for your own well-being. You are worth it, as you are the greatest asset to your pupils, far more important than a textbook or a worksheet. If you need someone to talk to for mental health or well-being support, you can contact the Education Support Partnership, on 08000 562 561 or visit www.educationsupport.org.uk/helping-you/telephone-support-counselling

# Further reading

If you are interested in the philosophical underpinning behind theories of performativity, read works by Jean-François Lyotard, Juliet Mitchell, Judith Butler, Jacques Derrida and Michel Foucault.

There are many blogs and online networks which have lots of resources and interaction facilities for teachers in their early career. You may like https://mrshumanities.com or https://earlycareer.chartered.college (accessed 18 August 2020).

Or on a lighter note, Davis, J L (2018) *DIY Circus Lab for Kids: A Family-Friendly Guide for Juggling, Balancing, Clowning, and Show-Making*. Beverley, MA: Quarto Publishing Group.

# References

Ball, S J (2012) Performativity, Commodification and Commitment: An I-Spy Guide to the Neoliberal University. *British Journal of Educational Studies*, 60(1): 17–28. [online] Available at: www.tandfonline.com/doi/full/10.1080/00071005.2011.650940 (accessed 14 September 2020).

Burnard, P and White, J (2008) Creativity and Performativity: Counterpoints in British and Australian Education. *British Educational Research Journal*, 34(5): 667–82. [online] Available at: www.jstor.org/stable/40375528 (accessed 14 September 2020).

Butler, J (2004) *Undoing Gender*. New York and London: Routledge.

CooperGibson Research/DfE (2018) *Factors Affecting Teacher Retention*. [online] Available at: https://assets.publishing.service.gov.uk/government/uploads/system/uploads/attachment_data/file/686947/Factors_affecting_teacher_retention_-_qualitative_investigation.pdf (accessed 14 September 2020).

Foster, D (2019) *Teacher Recruitment and Retention in England*. Briefing Paper Number 7222, 16 December 2019. London: House of Commons Library. [online] Available at: https://researchbriefings.files.parliament.uk/documents/CBP-7222/CBP-7222.pdf (accessed 14 September 2020).

Perryman, J and Calvert, G (2020) What Motivates People to Teach, and Why Do They Leave? Accountability, Performativity and Teacher Retention. *British Journal of Educational Studies*, 68(1): 3–23. [online] Available at: www.tandfonline.com/doi/abs/10.1080/00071005.2019.1589417?journalCode=rbje20 (accessed 14 September 2020).

Turner, R L and Denny, D A (1969) Teacher Characteristics, Teacher Behavior, and Changes in Pupil Creativity. *The Elementary School Journal*, 69(5): 265–70. [online] Available at: www.jstor.org/stable/1000924 (accessed 14 September 2020).

# Chapter 3  People like me

# What? (The big idea)

### '...To thine own self be true'

There is probably no better play than Shakespeare's *Hamlet* for examining the self. *'This above all, to thine own self be true'* (*Hamlet*, 1.3.77) is one of Shakespeare's wisest lines, spoken by Polonius to his son, Laertes, as he leaves for his 'gap year'. The quote sets the tone for this chapter, by encouraging you to have an honest discourse with yourself. You may not be familiar with the play, but suffice to know that the eponymous prince is angry with just about everyone and at war with himself throughout. Torn between loyalty, love, compassion and revenge, he is a good example of someone who is unsure of who they are, who they want others to think they are and what their role should be. Most schools don't have ramparts or ghosts, so it is probably safe to leave the likeness there, but prepare yourself for some soul-searching in the following tasks.

This chapter looks at teacher identity and how both the image and the reality of your teacher self impacts on your attitudes and approaches to your professional workload. It is important in the first instance to recognise that we are all capable of multiple identities. Are you an aunty? Are you a son? Are you a mother or a father? Would you describe your gender in binary terms or fluid? Are you a cook; a gardener; a cocktail mixologist or a vegetable zymologist? Do you pray; do you meditate; are you a talker or a listener? Already you can see that you can be a number of these at the same time, without confusion or compromise. So, can you have multiple aspects to your teacher identity too and can you draw on these diverse aspects at different times to meet differing situations? Are you a patient teacher, a loud instructor, a facilitator, a compassionate solver, or a goal attainer? There is an opportunity to look at this more closely later in the chapter, but first it is important to explore why teacher identity is important and how it may hold one of the keys to tackling your workload more effectively.

# So what? ◀ ◀ ◀

### 'To the manner born' (*Hamlet*, 1.4.15)

Many teachers cite their belief that they *'always wanted to teach'*, that they are *'really good with children'* and some that they feel a natural affinity with teaching, but these views cannot be sustained without success in the role. Through the narratives of early career teachers and trainees, Jennifer Nias (1989) demonstrated her belief that teaching calls for a *'massive investment of self'*. This 'self' is a complex dance between role, culture, identity and ideas of a teacher self, or teacher biography, that pre-date any training or practice. Teachers bring their institutionally formed biographies to their role. That is to say, their teaching styles are informed, consciously or unconsciously, by how they were taught at school – how their days were structured, what aspects of the curriculum were emphasised, how teachers made them feel – and so teachers arrive at the start of their career with a predetermined image of teaching (Britzman, 1986; Mayer, 1999). Even if that image is not always idealised, it is inherent and impacts on how they then teach. This teaching self then becomes the frame of reference, against which developing aspects of the teacher identity are tested. For example, classroom organisation is often hugely influenced by ideas of what a classroom has traditionally looked like throughout the teacher's own school experience. Notions of what 'worked for me as a learner' can be hard to challenge on a conscious level and even more difficult to examine if you are not open to which practices have influenced you from your own school days.

Because so much about school is familiar, it can be hard to acknowledge the emotional tension this can bring when the role is a lot harder than you imagined it to be, when you were looking at it from the other side of the desk, as a child.

> But while the situations are familiar, experiencing these tensions from the teacher's role is not. Indeed, the emotional world of the teacher is a new encounter. This is the difficult process of making sense of, and acting within, self-doubt, uncertainty, and the unexpected, while assuming a role which requires confidence, certainty, and stability. It is a painful experience, often carried out in a state of disequilibrium.
>
> (Britzman, 1986, p 452)

## 'To be, or not to be – that is the question' (Hamlet, 3.1.55)

Examining teacher identity exposes so many dichotomies. In examining your own teacher self, you should try to marry these diverse aspects, rather than allowing a conflictual approach, which will almost certainly overwhelm you. However, it is also important to note that the popular notion of teacher identity is based on how others see teachers, which in turn often shapes how you see yourself. The concept of teacher identity first became a separate area of research in the 1970s, but the origins of teacher identity are rooted in historical and sociological studies of the public education system. Many teachers in the nineteenth and early twentieth century were of working-class background and many were women, expected to live in social and economic dependence on their patrons and employers (Nias, 1997). There were long struggles for recognition, better pay and status, while being beholden to those who inspected, employed and paid them. These conditions led to habits of deference and dependency, which can still be found in the roots of the hierarchical systems in today's schools.

Finding a teacher identity that is not bound by habits of institutionally formed biography can be difficult. Walkington (2005) noted that experiences that can shape teacher beliefs and identity are often formed from atypical moments that created happy and lasting memories. These don't necessarily have any bearing on what happens day to day as a teacher. It's similar to Year 6 pupils always being allowed to experience the Bunsen burners on their transition visit to secondary school and then only at brief moments ever after in the actual lessons. However, their memory of chemistry will probably still involve a flame and a flask. So a memory of the class playing a trick on the geography teacher, who joins in with the joke and everyone laughs together, is a long way from the reality of planning a Year 10 global development module for a large, academically diverse group.

Walkington gathered observations from pre-service teachers from a series of brief classroom observations. The trainees noted attributes such as the teachers' patience and flexibility and remarked on the organisation, discipline and subject knowledge required. They referred to simplistic notions of teachers they observed as being *'good teachers'* or using *'good strategies'*. These visits were followed up with carefully structured sessions which used the mentoring relationship to build on these still shapeless impressions through discussion and reflection. Recognising the importance of the mentor role in this aspect of the early career teacher's development, Walkington notes: *'It is their personal philosophies of teaching which shape their emerging teaching identities'* (Walkington, 2005, p 59). A poorly trained mentor has the potential to 'shut down' dissenting views of a trainee. As a newly qualified teacher, for example, you may not have felt that you had the permission, or the skills, to offer critical reflection of your mentor's practice, or the practice of a colleague, but this may also have added to inherent feelings that your own ideas are 'wrong', which adds to your disenchantment and reduces any agency you feel. This only serves to highlight the importance of an effective and consultative mentor, who works with you as a trainee or early career teacher from the start to model, challenge, inform and concede on aspects of teacher identity and how this can relate to your future attitudes to workload. There is a strong argument for a *'pedagogy of becoming'*, which enables the mentor and mentee to work together, drawing on the new teacher's views of education and the foundation of the relationship as *'meaning-making and professional learning'* (Velikova, 2019, p 15, cited in Ivanova, 2020, p 37). If you have already had a good professional mentor within your experience, you will be able to reflect on how that has influenced your own teacher identity, but the very best mentoring will allow you to bring and shape your own views, even when the process is uncomfortable for either or both of you.

Studies across the world reflect how teacher identity is formed by the *'cumulative experience of school lives'* (Britzman, 1986) and subsequently, this identity impacts on the hopes and aspirations of the teacher's practice. Chong et al (2011) conducted research interviews with pre-service teachers in Singapore, three-quarters of whom were female and mostly in their twenties. Participants were asked to rate *'How I feel about teaching'* on a five-point Likert scale against the themes of: role of teaching and learning; self as a role model; sense of calling; sense of professional identity; professional growth as a teacher. These questions were asked at the entry and exit points of their training and the results showed that there were significant decreases in four areas. The trainees' *'belief in the value of teaching and learning'* generally stayed the same, but *'sense of calling'* showed the biggest decrease. This suggests that, too often, teachers are ill-prepared to harmonise the disparity between their hopeful, or dream teacher identity *('I'll be a teacher who can make a difference to children')* and the actual teacher identity *('I spend too many hours preparing data for managers that has no impact on my pupils')*. These findings are reflected in the Department for Education's own examination of teacher retention in the workforce in England (CooperGibson Research/DfE, 2018).

Kaplan and Garner (2017) propose the Dynamic Systems Model of Role Identity (DSMRI), which presents teacher learning as identity formation. They use a meta-theoretical framework that integrates a number of perspectives from contemporary theorists across disciplines, as well as *'empirical research on students' and teachers' contextual formation of environmental perceptions, self-perceptions, motivation, and action, e.g. choice, investment of effort, self-regulation'* (Garner and Kaplan, 2019, p 9). The dynamic element of the model, illustrated in Figure 3.1, is that it emphasises *'teacher identity as based in the personal version of the teacher role that a person construes within her or his lived context'* (p 9). Kaplan and Garner embrace the natural factors that impact on teachers and consider the interdependence of circumstances and other factors on a teacher's identity formation. It is not something that you can get 'off the shelf'; for example, you cannot guarantee a set teacher identity if you could just read this, watch that and do this. Myriad factors are in play from your childhood and while it is not possible to capture in a few lines, the illustration helps to explain the thinking behind Kaplan and Garner's DSMRI.

**Figure 3.1  The Dynamic Systems Model of Role Identity**
(Kaplan and Garner, 2017, p 2041)

The model shows the interdependence of the four main aspects of teacher identity and the factors that impact on them. '*Like in any other complex dynamic system, change in the teacher role identity is highly dependent on the system's state and on its environment, which includes the personal and professional contexts in which the teacher lives and works*' (Garner and Kaplan, 2019, p 10). You can almost see the circles in the figure expanding and contracting as your teacher self adapts to challenges, encounters momentary defeats and discovers new ideas.

Teacher identity is different from your teacher role, in which you generally become more confident as you develop your pedagogy, learn new skills and flex your professional muscles. Your teacher identity can be prone to '*slings and arrows*', many of which may be self-inflicted. A feeling that you are not in control of your workload can impact on your teacher identity and increase a sense of failure, even when this may be contrary to all the evidence in your classroom. Zembylas (2003, p 216) summarises Nias (1989, 1993, 1996) in observing that:

> *teachers invest their selves in their work and so they closely merge their sense of personal and professional identity. They invest in the values that they believe their teaching represents. Consequently, their teaching and their classroom become a main source for their self-esteem and fulfilment as well as their vulnerability.*

Recognising your teacher identity and being open to knowing more about your teacher self allows you to develop your strengths and perhaps put your childhood lens to one side. Using the tasks over the next few pages, and finding a trusted colleague or mentor who can work with and alongside you in a paired approach, you can develop an adult version of your teacher identity. It is an identity of which you can be proud and from which you can grow stronger and wiser, enabling you to take a professional approach to decisions about your role and workload.

## Reflective task ◀◀◀

### People like me

The words in the following reflective task can each describe a teacher self: for example, a compliant teacher; a dedicated teacher. Read through the words carefully and consider which words you might use to describe yourself as a teacher. Once you are familiar with all the adjectives, follow the instructions below the chart.

Because you are creating an auto biographical profile, remember that you cannot be objective in this exercise. You are you and you see you through your own eyes. Embrace that notion and be as honest as you can allow yourself to be, but don't use it as a tool to be unkind to yourself. If you get stuck with too many words you may feel uncomfortable with, what does that tell you about how you are feeling about your job at the moment?

| Compassionate | Hard hearted | Dispassionate | Emotional |
|---|---|---|---|
| Resilient | Defeatist | Tough | Pushover |
| Lazy | Lethargic | Energetic | Frantic |
| Static | Hands-on | Practical | Inept |
| Didactic | Laissez-faire | Facilitative | Over-supportive |
| Community minded | Collegiate | Independent | Team player |
| Practical | Pragmatic | Naïve | Idealistic |
| Flexible | Intransigent | Dedicated | Faithful |
| Flippant | Amusing | Easily amused | Serious |
| Moral | Honest | Indifferent | Authentic |
| Respectful | Unquestioning | Subversive | Enquiring |
| Dedicated | Casual | Committed | Responsive |
| Predictable | Creative | Resourceful | Innovative |
| Passive | Aggressive | Compliant | Competitive |
| Friendly | Companionable | Isolated | Shy |
| Effortless | Natural | Methodical | Artificial |
| Happy | Disappointed | Empty | Fulfilled |
| Anxious | Laid back | Reactive | Responsive |
| Accepting | Open | Challenging | Resistant |
| Radical | Liberal | Tolerant | Judgemental |
| Traditional | Inclusive | Provincial | Culturally enriching |

Use different coloured pens, or overlays.

1. Choose one from each row to describe the teacher you set out to be (a).

2. Choose one from each row to describe the teacher you feel you are today (b).

3. If your dream teacher self (a) is sufficiently distanced by time and experience from your actual teacher self (b), then also choose one from each row to describe the teacher you would still like to be by invoking your aspirational teacher self (c).

- What might be the reasons for some of the differences between (a) and (b)?

- What needs to change if there are differences between (b) and (c)?

- Are all your (a)'s the same as your (c)'s? What are the reasons for any differences?

- Where (a) and (b) are the same, how have you managed to achieve your dream self?

- Can you learn from this and apply the same reasoning to areas where there is now a bigger difference?

Leave it a couple of days and do your (b)'s again. Not all words in a row are exclusive of each other; you may find it hard to pick just one, but try to prioritise the one you feel most fits. How might your colleagues describe you? How might your pupils describe you? It is perfectly possible to be different things to many different people without that being harmful. It is part of being human that we can present in seemingly contradictory ways. It is normal to dislike the monotony of marking and feel indolent about the task, while at the same time feel energised and excited by seeing how the group you weren't working with have all applied their new understanding of ratio from the previous lesson. It is okay to be resistant to planning, but then enjoy being creative while designing a task that will enable the children to get to the heart of the objective. This is a task you can come back to over time and add to and adjust your reflections. Share with colleagues and discuss your similarities and differences. Take care not to be self-critical, but to use this as a framework for self-critique: the former is emotion intensive and the second is task intensive.

## Case study ◀◀◀

Heather is in her third year of teaching and has two small children under seven. Like so many teachers, she tussles with herself over whether she is good or not, skilled or not, confident or not. She has lacked good mentoring, but also seems happiest when she is left alone.

*I'd always wanted to teach, wanted to make a difference. I remember writing on my first teaching application form that I'd always wanted to work with children. It was true. It is true, but there is so much else that seems to get in the way and the strange thing is, my own children no longer get the best of me, because I'm always cross or grumpy when I get home – always tired, never feeling like I've finished for the day, or done a good job.*

*In my classroom, with the doors shut and just me and my class of children I can still be the teacher I wanted to be. I think I'm fair, kind, knowledgeable, even funny sometimes. I think I'm good at knowing when a different approach or strategy might work for an individual or group, but that is one of the things you don't ever really know – what works one day doesn't seem to work the next for some children.*

*I'm patient (until I'm not!). One child really knows what to do to set me on edge. I've had to work hard to understand why she might need my attention at times and how to pre-empt that when I can. I think I was being lazy putting all the blame on the child, but it was making me miserable and the child was becoming more and more to blame for everything in my head. The other teacher in my team just agreed that the child was the problem, so that kept it all going for a while, but then we got a new SENDCO and I found a website, 'Lives in the Balance', and it really helped me think about the teacher I would rather be. Finding ways to meet the needs of all the children in my class has made me feel more skilled. I'm still exhausted at the end of the day, but maybe I'm just blaming the job now, in the way I blamed the child. It would be good to know what I can do differently.*

# Now what?

Nias (1997, p 16) wrote: *'many teachers are most fulfilled by their work when they are most depleted by its demands'*. In speaking with hundreds of teachers and trainees through her research, she recognised the tussles that so many have between the role they set their hearts on at an early age and the reality of a demanding professional career. Not all teachers are early adopters of wanting to 'make a difference to children'; many more teachers now approach the position as a way of acquiring skills they can apply elsewhere. Indeed, the premise of teacher educators such as Teach First is to capitalise on the youthful skills of high-flying graduates to *'teach first, then do something else afterwards'*. No route into teaching has to result in the newly trained teacher having a fixed identity. Whatever their starting points, all teachers can be subject to Damascene conversions in any direction as a result of people, cultures and circumstances which influence them along the way. It is difficult not to be influenced by a school culture you find you love or hate, by children you teach who thrive or struggle, and by colleagues who support or hamper. But your teacher identity is yours and not anyone else's. Be true to yourself, keep asking yourself *'Why?'*, *'What?'*, *'How?'* and importantly, *'For whose benefit?'* To thrive professionally, you will need a good measure of your role that benefits your pupils, but also many elements that appeal to and benefit your own sense of teacher self.

## Practical task for tomorrow

*'There is nothing either good or bad, but thinking makes it so'*
**(Thompson and Taylor 2006, p 466)**

You can now use your knowledge of your teacher self more effectively in your professional approach to workload. Think about a task that can overwhelm you, such as report writing. There are many practical ways to approach this and colleagues with years of experience may be able to share the ways they break up the task and make it doable, but the doing of it, ultimately, has to be done! However, one strategy you can try is envisioning. At times, when you don't want to start a task you may be self-shaming, berating yourself for being lazy or indolent. Be kinder to yourself. Set yourself some time before the task is due to envisage yourself doing the thing you are trying to avoid doing. Find a time that is quiet and uncluttered; before you go to sleep, in the half-waking time of the early morning, lying in the bath, or five minutes before you turn on the television for your favourite programme. Close your eyes and imagine yourself writing a pupil's report. See the first page in your mind and envisage your cup of coffee by the side of your laptop and then signing the end of the report. Picture the pile of finished reports on your desk, ready to be given out. Try to balance positive images of the task as well as some of the functional aspects that you find more difficult. It is likely that, in your mind, you will see yourself looking out of a window, but draw your image back to you writing. You may need to do this several times before you start and you might need other motivational strategies alongside for an effort-intensive task, but it can be surprisingly effective. You still may not feel you are your teacher dream self, but it is using a dream-like state to your advantage.

## Practical task for next week ◀◀◀

*'You yourself shall have the key of it'* (*Hamlet*, 1.3.85)

Earlier in the chapter, emotions were proposed as the source of resistance or self-transformation. This is particularly pertinent in relation to how you approach your workload. Resistance is not always a negative behaviour, particularly if you are opposing a moral or ethical wrong, but it is useful to know which aspects of your teacher identity can become emotion-fuelled behaviours. It is also important to recognise which behaviours are constructive and which are destructive, particularly to those around you and to those you teach.

Thinking about the list of teacher attributes from the reflective task that form your ideal identity and your current teacher identity, draw out those that impact on how you approach your workload and use the following exercise to make some next steps. A key is a well-known symbol for finding solutions and this task can be applied in many different ways, so use it for yourself, but you can also adapt it to support your pupils to solve problems.

A key can open doors to positive change, but also lock doors, behind which you can leave things you no longer choose to do or see.

## Example ◀◀◀

| Doors you want to open | Doors you want to close |
|---|---|
| Opportunities to explore/practice to develop in your approach to workload. | Habits you wish to break/practice which is detrimental to your workload. |
| eg Be more honest with colleagues when I know I would benefit from planning by myself and not sitting together.<br><br>Suggest focused ten minutes each day to review pupil responses and agree next steps, but then plan by myself. | eg Put 'pushover me' behind the door! Learn to communicate 'no' effectively. |

## Practical task for the long term ◀◀◀

Consider ways to have more control over your teacher identity and your teacher attributes. Without spending too much time or over-thinking things, assign a teacher self to your lesson planning. For example, if you are planning a lesson on fractions and your pupils have been struggling to remember much from last year, write and circle 'methodical self' onto the plan. See if that helps to shape your approach to unpicking the misconceptions and interrupt the children's forgetting. If you are planning a French vocabulary test, then 'didactic self' may be appropriate, with a sprinkling of 'innovative self' as you try a new way of focusing the class consciousness prior to the test. You could ask each child to find a fixed point in the classroom, a poster or a door panel, and teach them how to use relaxing breathing while looking at the fixed point. Put the words due to come up in the test on the board and ask them to read each word in the test and then look at the fixed point they have chosen. Remove the words from the board and read them out in a different order. Remind the pupils that if they get stuck, look to their fixed point and see if they free their memory. It may help, it may not, but your 'enquiring self' can enjoy the challenge of testing this hypothesis.

If it helps, record in your journal when this approach of assigning teacher self is successful for you and when it isn't. Alternatively, you could return to your plan and put stars out of five by the teacher self you chose and talk to colleagues about what worked and what might work better next time.

# What next?

It is important not to leave this chapter without raising one more dichotomy in teacher identity, within the communal isolation of the role. As a teacher, your central professional relationship is with your class; individually and collectively. At points in the school day, you are surrounded by colleagues, parents and carers, and children, and yet there will be times when you will feel that you are alone, isolated, or even shipwrecked on an island in a sea of sharks.

If you are feeling overwhelmed, then try to remember that you are not alone. In truth you are surrounded by people who feel, or have felt, exactly the same as you. There are support networks for teaching professionals available too, such as Education Support.

Use the exercises in this chapter to celebrate the complexity of your teacher identity. Congratulate yourself on harnessing your beliefs, your institutional biography, your habits and all those influences in your culture and environment, to be your own type of teacher. But remember not to get stuck there. Developing, refining and evolving your teacher identity is a professional responsibility and you're going to be great!

## Further reading

Education Support – support for education professionals to manage work-life and workload. [online] Available at: www.educationsupport.org.uk/ (accessed 10 August 2020).

Lives in the Balance – resources and information from an organisation based in Maine, the United States, to support educators to meet the needs of young people with social, emotional and mental health needs. [online] Available at: www.livesinthebalance.org/ (accessed 18 August 2020).

Schools in Mind – well-being resources from the Anna Freud National Centre for Children and Families. [online] Available at www.annafreud.org/what-we-do/schools-in-mind/resources-for-schools/supporting-staff-wellbeing-in-schools/ (accessed 18 August 2020).

Shakespeare, W. *Hamlet: Prince of Denmark.*

# References

Britzman, D (1986) Cultural Myths in the Making of a Teacher: Biography and Social Structure in Teacher Education. *Harvard Educational Review*, 56(4): 442–56. [online] Available at: www.hepg.org/her-home/issues/harvard-educational-review-volume-56,-issue-4/herarticle/biography-and-social-structure_498 (accessed 20 June 2020).

Chong, S, Low E L and Goh K C (2011) Developing Student Teachers' Professional Identities: An Exploratory Study. *International Education Studies*, 4(1): 30–9. [online] Available at: https://eric.ed.gov/?id=EJ1066392 (accessed 25 June 2020).

CooperGibson Research/DfE (2018) *Factors Affecting Teacher Retention*. [online] Available at: https://assets.publishing.service.gov.uk/government/uploads/system/uploads/attachment_data/file/686947/Factors_affecting_teacher_retention_-_qualitative_investigation.pdf (accessed 14 September 2020).

Garner, J and Kaplan, A (2019) A Complex Dynamic Systems Perspective on Teacher Learning and Identity Formation: An Instrumental Case. *Teachers and Teaching*, 25(1): 7–33. [online] Available at: www.tandfonline.com/doi/full/10.1080/13540602.2018.1533811 (accessed 27 June 2020).

Ivanova, I (2020) Strengthening Teacher Identity and Professionalism as a Way to Increase the Appeal and Status of Teaching Profession. *Studies in Linguistics, Culture and FLT*, 6. [online] Available at: www.researchgate.net/publication/341265969 (accessed 14 September 2020).

Kaplan, A and Garner, J K (2017) A Complex Dynamic Systems Perspective on Identity and its Development: The Dynamic Systems Model of Role Identity. *Developmental Psychology*, 53(11): 2036–51. [online] Available at: https://psycnet.apa.org/buy/2017-48409-004 (accessed 25 June 2020).

Mayer, D (1999) *Building Teaching Identities: Implications for Pre-service Teacher Education.* Paper presented to the Australian Association for Research in Education, Melbourne. [online] Available at: www.aare.edu.au/data/publications/1999/may99385.pdf (accessed 24 June 2020).

Nias, J (1989) *Primary Teachers Talking: A Study of Teaching and Work*. London: Routledge.

Nias, J (1997) Would Schools Improve if Teachers Cared Less? *Education*, 25(3): 3–13. [online] Available at: www.tandfonline.com/doi/abs/10.1080/03004279785200291 (accessed 24 June 2020).

Thompson, A and Taylor, N (eds) (2006) *The Arden Shakespeare: Hamlet*. London: Cengage Learning.

Walkington, J (2005) Becoming a Teacher: Encouraging Development of Teacher Identity Through Reflective Practice. *Asia-Pacific Journal of Teacher Education*, 33(1): 53–64. [online] Available at: www.tandfonline.com/doi/pdf/10.1080/1359866052000341124 (accessed 17 June 2020).

Zembylas, M (2003) Emotions and Teacher Identity: A Poststructural Perspective. *Teachers and Teaching: Theory and Practice*, 9(3). [online] Available at: www.tandfonline.com/doi/pdf/10.1080/13540600309378 (accessed 14 September 2020).

# Chapter 4    Choose your words

# What? (The big idea)

## The language of agency

From an early age, children are taught to do as they are told; to conform and to comply with adult direction. Fairy tales and children's stories warn of the perils of independent thinking, curiosity and controlling behaviours. Think of Max in *Where the Wild Things Are*; consider Angry Arthur, or Alice in Wonderland. There are always exceptions to this rule, but even in books such as *Matilda* the heroine aspires to a gentle life of books and learning, far away from the successes of her free thinking which had enabled her to expose the abuses at home and at school. These stories add to the cacophony of messages that impact on cultural norms, affecting perceptions of gender, identity and diversity, for example. These messages, over time and through the discourse that follows, contribute to how you feel about your place in the world and your ability to make change.

Having agency in the decisions about your own life and in your own workplace is a good thing, but in the context of schools (which are managerially hierarchical) having a say can be seen as subversive, conflictual and unhelpful. Those who offer opinions that are contrary to the status quo are sometimes deemed 'meddlers', 'trouble' or 'bolshy'. It would seem fair that if a school development plan had been agreed and a member of staff was constantly questioning the direction of travel, the practice and procedures of the school, in a way that was critical, personal or affected the quality of provision for the children in that teacher's class, then a particular type of professional conversation would need to be held in which the teacher's own approach and practice could be challenged. However, all too often in schools, critique is confused with criticism; questioning with subversion; making an argument with being argumentative; and discourse with dispute. The language of agency is so important and is intrinsically tied to emotional capital.

This chapter enables you to explore teacher agency and develop your thinking about forms of capital, so that you can be part of creating a more effective and collegial approach to policy, procedure and practice in education, particularly in relation to your workload.

Biesta et al (2015, p 624) describe teachers' agency as '*their active contribution to shaping their work and its conditions – for the overall quality of education*'. They recognise that agency is not a property, capacity or competence, but something that people do. As a result, the quality of someone's agency is not down to the individual, but is dependent on the quality of their engagement with '*temporal – relational contexts-for-action*'. Emirbayer and Mische (1998) proposed this phrase while defining agency in sociological and historical perspectives. It describes how your level of agency is affected by the past, present and future as you navigate between them in your considerations, actions and reflections; employing your ability to simultaneously hold your own views while considering the views of others and navigating overlapping needs and demands arising from the interplay with habit, imagination and judgement. Quite complex then! Biesta et al argue that teachers' agency is heavily influenced by factors which are often beyond their immediate control. As you may already have discovered, it can be quite difficult for an early career teacher to demonstrate their own agency for change, but this can also be true for many longstanding teachers. However, difference can be achieved in the small things, even if you can't always impact directly on the big things. If you want to achieve a professionally acceptable workload, then it helps to know how you can make change. Having clarity about your teacher identity, your beliefs and philosophy of education on the one hand, while on the other developing confidence in your learned skills, characteristics, knowledge and experience (such as the intended purpose and preferable pedagogy for each lesson) can be powerful tools in equipping you to have agency in the decisions which affect you.

However, any discussion of teacher workload is affected by the relationship between a teacher's role and responsibilities and their emotional response to the work that is involved. Layered into this is the teacher's understanding of the feelings and attitudes of colleagues and parents/carers to that work and the policies and practices that relate to it, as decided by senior managers, governors and government. All this is balanced by how much the teacher feels they have agency over this work. The potential for a deficit of emotional capital, when people feel they have no control over work demands, also applies if people feel disempowered to make the changes needed to improve working conditions (Daly and Greer, 2019).

## Creep mouse!

In the childhood game of creep mouse, the participants creep up on the 'cat' and freeze on the spot when the cat spins around to glare, powerless under the gaze of the cat and only able to move when the cat is not looking. If the cat spots you moving then you are punished by going back to the beginning, reinforcing its power. Only by stealth and subterfuge can a mouse win the game. You are unlucky if that acts as an analogy for the power structures in your school, but there are several ways in which teachers are coerced into workload in ways that leave them without agency and without a voice.

Interruptions are an unforeseen way in which someone adds to your workload. Many managers may not even be aware that they do it, as Milliken and Dunn-Jensen (2005) found that managers' interrupting behaviour often increases when they are under pressure for a deadline, such as an imminent inspection. Interrupting instructions are often given in passing, but with plenty of emotional capital on the part of the instructor and no suggestion that this can't be done: '*Hi, I know it's your PPA time, but you're good at techy things, could you just go and see Claire, as she needs some help with her whiteboard*'. With a '*Thank you*' added if you're lucky.

But interrupting is a two-fold problem:

> *First, when a manager interrupts with a request, the work requested is added to the current workload, adding on tasks to the individual's job. Second, interruptions have the effect of detracting from the worker's efficiency at accomplishing the first task because there are significant costs associated with having to go back and try to remember where one was when one was interrupted... Interruptions, thus, contribute to the expansion of work hours in two ways: by adding tasks and by creating inefficiency in the accomplishment of current tasks.*
>
> (Milliken and Dunn-Jensen, 2005, p 47)

Work creep is an interesting concept in relation to your perception of workload. It is anomalous in that you would appear to have the agency in this, and yet it rarely seems like it. The next chapter on balancing your professional work and home life explores this further, but, in brief, work creep is where the measures and outcomes of performative work mean that it can be easier to undertake one more lesson plan before you cook supper, one more email before you put the children to bed, one more... It's not that you don't put your home life and family first, it is just that you can justify putting them second. Watch out for this!

Some tasks just do have to be done, so it is important to work out whether you feel denied of agency in relation to a task, or whether this is something that is part of your role and makes a difference to the children you teach and therefore there is no battle to be fought here.

Although teachers' actions are important within any discussion of agency, so much emotional capital is exchanged through spoken language. The vocabulary used in education and in your classroom and staffroom in particular is vital for empowering and for disempowering. The tasks in this chapter enable you to take better ownership of the language of workload and claim the capital within the words.

# So what? ◀ ◀ ◀

## The language of Bourdieu

The French sociologist Pierre Bourdieu helped to establish the current thinking on forms of capital. Although he did not write specifically about emotional capital, his writing on social and cultural capital enabled scholars to build on these notions to explore other forms of human capital.

In a very thin nutshell, Bourdieuian theory applied to education may look like this.

» Our 'field' is the social setting in which we operate, which may overlap; eg Initial Teacher Education, a classroom, or staffroom.

» Our 'habitus' is the structure in which we have internalised all the influences on us from home, family, friends and society and which form our unknowing reactions and responses within the field(s) in which we operate as social beings.

» Our 'capital' is *"that 'energy of social physics"... in all its different forms'* (Bourdieu and Wacquant, 1992, p 118): economic capital (student loan, bank of mum and dad); social capital (who we know, how they help or hinder us); cultural capital (what we know, how we use that to our advantage or how it disadvantages us).

» Our 'doxa' are the rules of the habitus: the commonly agreed policies of the school and unwritten rules of the school community, eg *'We don't take hot drinks onto the playground'* and *'We don't go onto the playground unless it is our duty'*.

All forms of capital involve an exchange of assets: I have something which is useful to someone else and, in return, that someone else will give me something. So, an example of financial capital is when you calculate you have enough money to exchange for goods you want and the vendor is happy with the amount you are willing to give.

An example of social capital is when you have friends or acquaintances with whom you can connect and, through them, connect to others. This also requires you to have enough social skills to be friendly, likeable or trusted and to communicate what you require. You may have shared values or something else in common that allows that initial interaction, but if you have social capital then you can build on this to create larger or more effective networks.

Cultural capital describes the advantage that can be gained by the exchange of knowledge or shared habits. You may have a really good knowledge of the Japanese artist Yayoi Kusama, so you introduce someone else to your favourite painting by this artist. In return, the person to whom you are talking begins to see you as someone who knows about art and invests in you other qualities that they associate with a person who is 'cultured'. In return, they may share their interest in something that is new to you, such as a new insight, book or gallery.

In the context of schools and colleges, a teacher's emotional capital is dependent on the ability to understand your own feelings and the feelings of others and to use that empathy effectively within the workplace as a resource through which to communicate to others how those feelings have been useful. Cottingham (2016, p 452) describes emotional capital as *'a tripartite concept composed of emotion-based knowledge, management skills, and capacities to feel that links self-processes and resources to group membership and social location'*.

## I think she's got it!

George Bernard Shaw's play, *Pygmalion*, written in 1912, light-heartedly and ironically shows how a young flower seller, Eliza Doolittle, could be taught to acquire enough accent (social capital) and knowledge of customs and habits of the upper classes (cultural capital) to pass for a duchess. Before Henry Higgins, the phonetician, offers these lessons for free, Eliza announces that she has saved enough of her flower seller income to pay for elocution lessons, so she can elevate her position to get a job in a flower shop. This is an example of financial capital, while showing that she has the intrinsic motivation to develop herself. Through much of the play Eliza has very little emotional capital; her wailing and her crying are shown to be ineffectual emotions in achieving any power or change. Although the play has some unfortunate inferences about power and permissions for a contemporary audience, the final scenes show Eliza has agency in her own future, as she takes ownership of the forms of capital she has attained and uses this knowingly and of her own volition.

### Goldilocks empowered

Taking a large literary leap into a fairy tale now, the story of *Goldilocks and the Three Bears* illustrates what happens when someone with little capital of any kind gets into a right old mess in a stranger's cottage. Goldilocks' behaviour is generally perceived by generations of young readers as spoilt, impolite, uncaring, unempathetic and greedy. But when woken by the bears from her sleep in the smallest bear's bed, she feels she has no option but to jump out of the window and evade capture. Can you imagine how the story might be different if Goldilocks had plenty of social, cultural and emotional capital?

'*Who's been sleeping in my bed?!*' Baby Bear would still cry, but Goldilocks might then answer with:

'*Hi! Oh my goodness! I didn't realise this was your house. You're the Oldberry Bear family, aren't you? I've heard so much about you. We were only talking about you last week. I'm great friends with the Newberry Bears in the village. I think they are your cousins, is that right? I'm Goldilocks, so lovely to meet you!*'

There's no guarantee the bears would be placated by this show of social capital, but it stands a better chance of easing the situation than a 12 foot drop out of the window!

- Can you think of some more examples of speech that would demonstrate forms of capital, which Goldilocks could exchange for extricating herself from her predicament?

Goldilocks could demonstrate she has cultural capital to use to her advantage here by saying:

'*I love what you've done with this room. The linen on the beds is fabulous. Is it Egyptian cotton? So beautifully soft. And your quilts are so intricate. Have you been to the American Museum in Bath? They have hundreds of beautiful family quilts. You would love them.*'

An example of emotional capital may be: '*I'm so sorry. I can see you are all feeling outraged by me lying in your bed. I do understand why you would be cross. I know there is no excuse for my behaviour, but please tell me what you need me to do to make it up to you. I've never done anything like this before.*'

For this to be authentic emotional capital, Goldilocks would need to genuinely feel these emotions and feel confident enough to share her feelings with the bears in exchange for empathy or sympathy. If she just said those things to try to get herself out of trouble, it would be easy to see through and unlikely to have the same value or worth and so less likely to be effective.

It can be easy to notice someone being manipulative, but in truth, humans manoeuvre and manipulate each other all the time. It is likely that when we notice the manipulation it is only when the person is not very skilled at getting others to do what they want, or perhaps when they are not genuine in their intent.

Think about this notion. Listen out for how people use speech to bring others round to their way of thinking, or to perform tasks they want doing. When does this rile you? When do you agree to do something willingly? Why do you react differently to some requests than to others? Do you react differently to some people than others? Can the same person encourage you to take on a task and then annoy you by asking you to complete a different task? Is the difference sometimes in yourself and how you are feeling at the time?

## Case study ◀◀◀

### The language of exclusion

There will be many times when you have felt powerless and lacking in any agency within your role. Colleagues and senior managers in particular can (both deliberately and inadvertently) use spoken and non-verbal language to reduce your agency. This in turn can impact on your well-being and affect your motivation, leaving you feeling that you are less likely to succeed.

Heather is an NQT, but had already had a lot of experience working with pupils with social, emotional and mental health needs. She felt frustrated by the way senior managers reacted to the sometimes challenging behaviour of a child in her first class, as senior staff would frequently come in to her room and 'take over', even though the child's behaviour often escalated as a result of someone coming into the class. Heather felt this often caused distress to the child and stress for her and added to her workload.

> Initially, I had gone to the deputy head asking for support and a plan for managing the difficult behaviour. As a result of this meeting, the child was removed from class, given ultimatums, threats of exclusion, and little emotional and academic support. It suddenly felt out of my hands. While some people might feel relieved to have SLT step in to remove a child displaying unsafe behaviour from class, it made me feel as though I were failing the child. This now felt like another mental load on top of my growing workload.

*Having previously worked in behaviour management, I wrote up a potential plan for the child, including a way of easing him back into class and re-building positive relationships. I approached the same deputy and was met with, 'We are handling it, you don't need to be involved', as a response. It felt like my opinion wasn't valued because I had asked senior managers for help in the first place. I felt frustrated that what had felt like a productive use of time was unnecessary. I decided to email my plan to all of SLT and my NQT mentor because I sincerely believed it was meaningful and could have a positive impact on a child's learning experience. I was relieved to see parts of my plan implemented, but I know it was a gamble and I was made to feel I had crossed a line, even though I couldn't specifically say they did this or that – it was just how I was made to feel.*

# Now what?

## Owning the language

Developing an understanding of your own feelings in relation to your workload is a theme you have been working on through these chapters, but these next tasks will help you to see how this understanding relates to emotional capital and agency. Remember, teacher agency is not intrinsic to you; it comes about through ongoing development of your beliefs and identity, an engagement with those around you (in your immediate environment and beyond), the ways in which your past, present and future can influence your thinking and your interaction with the systems within which you work. The better you truly know yourself as a teacher, perhaps the more agency you are likely to have to make your own choices about your workload.

A demonstration of your understanding of yourself and your emotions can come from your use of language and your ability to reflect on how language is used around you and how you use and develop language yourself.

## Practical task for tomorrow

### Goldilocks reformed!

Return to Goldilocks and think how she would have behaved in the bears' house had she had a better understanding of agency. As you go about your day in school tomorrow, use the line below to mark each exchange with another adult. For example, if a senior colleague asks you to take on an extra playtime duty with a moment's notice, you may feel you had no agency and it made you feel quite heated. Mark this at the 'hot' end, as you care a lot about your lack of agency. However, if you recognise you have no choice in doing the duty, but actually you quite like being outside and it means you do actually get to have a break (if you stay in your classroom you'll just carry on marking) then you may mark it down the 'cold' end. If, when the member of staff asks you to do the duty, you are able to say, '*Yes, happy to do that; I'll ask Tim to start my class off with their spelling task when they come in, so I can nip to the loo*', then you may feel that you have employed some agency within this situation and your mark is hovering around the 'just right' centre. If you feel able to use this as a stimulus for professional conversation with a mentor or colleague, make sure that individual colleagues are not distinguishable on the chart.

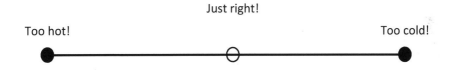

Just right!

Too hot!                                                                    Too cold!

## Practical task for next week ◀◀◀

### Language of emotional capital

You have started thinking about the language you use in the workplace and how this impacts on your emotional responses to your workload. Over the next week, listen carefully to the language that is used around you (received) and by you (communicated to others). In a way that doesn't breach anyone else's privacy, try to record the phrases that are used within school and collate them into positive and negative exchanges.

Some examples of emotional capital and their potential forms of exchange.

| Negative exchange | | Positive exchange | |
| --- | --- | --- | --- |
| **Received** | **Communicated** | **Received** | **Communicated** |
| *'I know you're feeling overworked at the moment, but we do just need this by Friday.'* | *'I've come in to work this morning, but I really don't feel well...'* | *'Would you be able to work on this more easily from home or in school?'* | *'I have found this quite hard to make sense of. Would you be able to go through it with me again?'* |
| *'You don't mind doing this for me, do you?'*<br><br>*'I've been feeling so stressed all night, after you told me how upset you were after that incident yesterday.'* | *'I know you would have been able to get this done in a few minutes, but it literally took me hours.'* | *'What seems a reasonable timeframe?'*<br><br>*'This has really played on my mind; how are you feeling about it?'* | *'I am feeling very anxious in the mornings in the staffroom briefings and there may be days when I struggle to come in. Can I talk to you about how to manage this better?'* |

You can collect your own examples here.

| Negative exchange | | Positive exchange | |
| --- | --- | --- | --- |
| **Received** | **Communicated** | **Received** | **Communicated** |
| | | | |

A negative exchange of emotional capital occurs when the owner does the giving and the taking. For example, offering an insight into how you might be feeling and then ignoring or negating those emotions. The positive exchanges show more empathy and reflection. Everyone is capable of using emotional capital for a negative exchange – you will probably catch yourself doing it with close friends or family far too frequently! But, within your professional field you can learn to exchange negative thoughts for positive words and notice how this changes your relationships with colleagues across the school structure.

Taking each negative exchange one at a time, consider how you might convert this into positive words, eg *'I feel really bad, but I really don't think I will be able to complete this by tomorrow!'* becomes *'I concentrate much better at home; I would like to leave at the same time as the children today and complete this task ready for tomorrow'* or *'I am aware of my deadline for this week, so I have planned for active marking in literacy, which I have recorded on SeeSaw for each child as I've gone along, so I can finish my task after school'*.

Acknowledge your feelings, or the feelings of others, and then propose a positive action.

**Thought converter. Think, reflect, communicate.**

## Practical task for the long term ◀◀◀

Share some of your thinking from this chapter with your mentor or a trusted colleague. Ask if you can build in discussions about agency into your regular meetings. Remember there are ethics of opposition and there will be times when you think you are being bold but come over as bossy, when you intended to be brave but misjudged it as brazen. These skills take time and reflection to get your professional tone just right. Like learning to sing, you can learn the melody and the lyrics, but you also have to get the timing right and develop the timbre of your voice. To sing well you need a good voice coach; to teach well you need to have a skilled mentor. If you don't have a mentor who supports you to become the best teacher you are capable of, summon up your courage and the skills you have been learning in this chapter to explore ways to find a mentor who matches you. Make an appointment to talk with the headteacher, write down what you want to say and remember to project positive emotional capital. However, occasionally, it may be that you find your best mentor beyond your own school's walls, through a friend or family member. If that's the only way it can work for a while, remember that's not cheating or being disempowered: it's doing what you need to do. If you wanted to sing professionally, you wouldn't think twice about finding a voice coach outside of working hours.

# What next?

In researching teacher agency, Biesta et al (2015) noticed that those teachers who lacked agency did not have access to a '*systematic set of professional discourses over and above those provided by the language of policy*'. They concluded that this contributed to the teachers' lack of agency by '*limiting their potential to envisage different futures, and through denying them the language with which to engage critically with policy*' (p 636).

Returning to the notion that agency comes from that layered interaction with identity, beliefs, time and relational structures, the absence of professional discourse holds the danger of fixing a teacher's beliefs and identity within their own past. An alternative risk may be in limiting the teacher's beliefs solely within their current school culture, which may or may not be conducive to positive professional growth. Without constructive mentoring, a teacher's existing beliefs are not experienced as choices, but appear inevitable.

> *Access to wider discourses about teaching and education would provide teachers with a perspective on the beliefs they and their colleagues hold, and would provide a horizon against which such beliefs can be evaluated. This is one important reason why we think that access to robust professional discourses about teaching does matter for teacher agency, and thus should be an important dimension of teacher education and further professional development.*
>
> (Biesta et al, 2015, p 638)

Having an ongoing and robust professional discourse is important for all teachers, but particularly in your early career. Indeed, all schools should be under a moral obligation to ensure early career teachers have access to trained mentors who have an understanding of the discourse around workload and its implications and that this is built into ongoing professional conversations and performance management processes.

# Further reading

Greer, J and Daly, C (2020) Professionally Acceptable Workload: Learning to Act Differently Towards Effective Change. *Impact*, 9. London: Chartered College of Teaching. Available at: https://impact.chartered.college/article/professionally-acceptable-workload-learning-act-differently-effective-change/ (accessed 14 September 2020). Caroline Daly is Professor of Teacher Education at the UCL Institute of Education.

Read George Bernard Shaw's *Pygmalion*. [online] Available at: www.gutenberg.org/files/3825/3825-h/3825-h.htm (accessed 18 August 2020). The last section of Shaw's narrative future-ending for the characters in his play makes for interesting reading in the light of the discourse on agency and capital.

While George Cukor's 1965 adaptation of Shaw's *Pygmalion* into the film *My Fair Lady* makes fine viewing for many reasons, it has a different ending from the play on which it was based. Enjoy watching it, but the original play provides a better insight to support your understanding of social and cultural capital.

Cheryl Reynolds' *Simple Introduction to Bourdieu* (2014) is an excellent animation explaining the language of Bourdieu in relation to capital. Reynolds is based at the University of Huddersfield. [online] Available at: www.youtube.com/watch?v=1W_IkfGg2nU&list=UUg_4z_8AM7x9wmZ6F1vJTcw&index=22 (accessed 18 August 2020).

# References

Biesta, G, Priestley, M and Robinson, S (2015) The Role of Beliefs in Teacher Agency. *Teachers and Teaching*, 21(6): 624–40. [online] Available at: doi.org/10.1080/13540602.2015.1044325 (accessed 10 July 2020).

Bourdieu, P and Wacquant, L (1992) *An Invitation to Reflexive Sociology*. Chicago, IL: University of Chicago Press.

Cottingham, M (2016) Theorizing Emotional Capital. *Theory and Society*, 45(5): 451–70.

Daly, C and Greer, J (2019) *Professionally Acceptable Workload: A Second UCET Companion*. London: UCET. [online] Available at: www.ucet.ac.uk/11213/professionally-acceptable-workload-a-second-ucet-companion-october-2019 (accessed 12 July 2020).

Emirbayer, M and Mische, A (1998) What Is Agency? *American Journal of Sociology*, 103(4): 962–1023. [online] Available at: www.jstor.org/stable/10.1086/231294 (accessed 12 July 2020).

Milliken, F J and Dunn-Jensen, L M (2005) The Changing Time Demands of Managerial and Professional Work: Implications for Managing the Work-Life Boundary. In Kossek, E E and Lambert, S J (eds) *Work and Life Integration: Organizational, Cultural, and Individual Perspectives* (pp 43–59). Mahwah, NJ: Lawrence Erlbaum Associates Publishers.

Shaw, G B (2003) *Pygmalion*. London: Penguin Classics.

# Chapter 5    A life in balance

## What? (The big idea)

### Have you ever balanced a spoon on your nose?

A dictionary definition of the word *balance* will offer you several choices, including a verb which describes finding a steady position, so that an object or person doesn't fall, or a noun in which at least two things are equal. If you are asked to propose a visual metaphor for balance in relation to work and life, or work and family, you may well suggest a set of scales, or a plank angled horizontally across a fulcrum. Most online searches for work–life balance will take you in a similar direction, with the occasional addition of the tightrope walker with a long cane. But these images don't really conjure up the complexity of the balancing acts you will need to perform throughout your teaching career. If you have ever balanced a spoon on your nose, you will know it takes some practice and a little skill, but in achieving it you quickly realise you can do very little else at the same time without risking the spoon falling off. It can be very similar when you contrive to find ways to balance your teaching role and the rest of your life. Just when you think you have found an effective way to balance your workload and your non-work life, something else crops up, like huge vet bills, or a relationship crisis, and everything seems to be out of kilter again.

Sharing their research on how to make 3D-printed shapes balance in precarious ways, Prévost et al (2013, p 1) note: '*Imbalance suggests a feeling of dynamism and movement in static objects. It is therefore not surprising that many 3D models stand in impossibly balanced configurations*'. This seems to be a good place to start this chapter on aspiring to a life in balance; that there can be an energy and vibrancy in imbalance. The nuance in this notion is that things may look imbalanced, but if you feel in control of the choices you have made and they are effective for you and those around you, then you may have achieved a perfectly imbalanced-balance – think more of the impossible beauty of a standing tyrannosaurus rex and less about those fine proportions of the thoroughbred race horse! There is a danger in pursuing the 'perfect' life in balance, as no such model life exists in a way which is transferable from one person to another. The blueprint for your life in balance will be bespoke, temporal and relational. This chapter is aimed at helping you to look at your choices and commitments in a way that will support you to find your own balance at this particular stage of your career, giving you the tools to adjust your plans at different times while considering the impact on those around you, including the children in your class.

## Have you ever tried to balance inequality?

Definitions of work–life balance vary in context (who is included and when) and content (what is included and how), but now generally apply to all genders. However, women across the ages have traditionally juggled a variety of roles, including within a workplace. The Industrial Revolution brought new challenges and demands on workers and pressure to ameliorate working conditions resulted in Victorian legislation as early as 1847, which attempted to reduce the hours that could be worked in textile factories to ten per day and five and a half on Saturdays (Parratt, 1998). This predominantly impacted on women and children as the largest workforce in textiles, but as subsequent laws extended to wider industries, conditions remained largely unregulated by too few inspectors and rules on hours were easily broken, ignored or even relaxed, particularly for women, who often worked in less regulated occupations, such as laundry and needlework. Incidentally, there are some interesting parallels with many sweat-shop occupations throughout the world today, with advantage being taken of those who have little voice. By the turn of the twentieth century, unionised male workers benefitted from hours which were on average two hours shorter per day than women, even in the most regulated occupations. While only one in ten married women were engaged in work in the late nineteenth and early twentieth centuries, some textile mills in the north-east encouraged married women to work. For unmarried working young women, there would also have been other caring and domestic roles within their households too: cleaning, darning, sewing; all aspects of the day to be fitted in and managed. While there is evidence that real wages increased for many during this time and leisure activities became more commodified, the ongoing fight for better working conditions was more visceral than pursuing a question of balance. But, as long hours and workload are among the reasons cited by former teachers for leaving the profession (Foster, 2019), it is important to recognise that achieving a life that feels balanced and fulfilling, while protecting your mental health and well-being, is the modern way of fighting for your employment rights.

The modern curiosity to understand work and family as a balancing act came about in the last three decades of the twentieth century. As equality acts enabled women to achieve long fought for status within the workplace, they were still maintaining predominant responsibility for the caring roles within the home. Into the twenty-first century there have been further changes both culturally and in legislation, such as shared parental leave and pay since 2015, which mean that juggling work and family, for instance, is no longer as gendered an issue as in the past. However, recent research in response to the coronavirus global pandemic has shown that where parents have both been working from home, due to lockdown and risk reduction restrictions, women in the UK have taken on more of the caring and coping roles in families during this time.

*During the first weeks of lockdown (28 March to 26 April 2020), in households with children aged under 18 years, women were carrying out on average two-thirds more of the childcare duties per day than men.*

*Women were delivering an average of 3 hours and 18 minutes of childcare, which includes time spent supervising children, while men contributed 2 hours.*

(Office for National Statistics, 2020)

The data shows that while developmental activities with children, such as reading or completing online learning, were generally evenly distributed between males and females, non-developmental roles on behalf of children, such as cleaning, washing and cooking, were more likely to be undertaken by women than men. There is no doubt that achieving a balance within your working life is as much of a challenge for men as women, but it is important to recognise that the source of these challenges may be different.

The tradition of considering work–life or work–family balance also needs to be broadened in relation to teachers in their early careers. While many who are new to teaching may have caring roles for their own children, others will be juggling diverse priorities, such as pets, team sports activities, leisure, charitable or volunteering interests. Some may also have caring responsibilities for people with disabilities or long-term illness. Akobo and Stewart (2020) concur with the need to embrace considerations of non-family households. They researched the experiences of work–life balance for women of African origin in the UK. They examined factors such as cultural sensitivities, personality types, financial commitments and government policies, and how these influence the conceptual views of work–family balance, job satisfaction and career progression. Their work is important in considering the diverse challenges for individuals of minority groups within the United Kingdom.

Education Support's (2020) 'Well-being wheel' recognises the multiple factors that are at play for individuals to achieve a sense of balance. They identify ten areas:

1. *money and finance;*

2. *career and work;*

3. *health and fitness;*

4. *fun and recreation;*

5. *friends;*

6. *environment (the environment you live, work or spend time in);*

7. *family;*

8. *partner and love;*

9. *growth and learning;*

10. *spirituality.*

Consider someone who is teaching full time, working beyond their directed time in term time and then training for and playing county-level hockey at the weekends. This teacher is also keeping in close contact with a school friend with a life-threatening condition and has close links to the local Gurdwara. This teacher may well need additional spokes to their wheel, which the toolkit does allow for, but it may not be as easy to compartmentalise the different aspects of life. Once you begin to look at a non-binary way of understanding all the competing and conflicting parts of your life, it gets a lot more complicated than a set of scales with 'work' on one side and 'life' on the other. Professional discourse and consultative mentoring can support you to make sense of this. For example, Akobo and Stewart propose that women of black, Asian and minority ethnic communities *'use internal and external networks as support systems'* (2020, p 147). The Black, Asian and Minority Ethnic Educators (BAMEed) network is a good example of an external support organisation.

For many teachers at the start of their career, work can be exhilarating and positively challenging. If this is you, the difference between life and work may be more blended, as you will explore later in this chapter in the reflective activity.

## Have you ever balanced books on your head?

*Work–life balance is the individual perception that work and non-work activities are compatible and promote growth in accordance with an individual's current life priorities.*

(Kallaith and Brough, 2008, p 326)

Like a lesson in deportment (balancing books on your head while holding yourself tall and proud), achieving a life in balance is defined by contemporary researchers as an individual task. In considering work–life balance, Kelliher et al (2017) promote a subjective, 'situationist' approach, rather than trying to attain equal distribution between aspects of life and work, often based on generalised assumptions. They recognise work–life balance as the relationship between work and non-work aspects of an individual's life, '*where achieving a satisfactory work-life balance is normally understood as restricting one side (usually work), to have more time for the other*' (p 98). Drawing on the work of Kallaith and Brough, Kelliher et al note that a subjectivist approach validates individual perceptions and allows for you and your colleague to have very different interpretations of work–life balance, while each can be appropriate and possible. Teachers who live without dependent family members may feel that their need for responsive and flexible solutions to work–life collisions are not as recognised as the more visible needs of parents or carers. As an early career teacher, it is important for you to know that your needs are recognised too, even if there isn't always a workable solution. There may be times when you will have to speak about issues that are making it hard for you to find an effective balance, as otherwise senior managers are unlikely to know that your flat has a moth infestation which has to be sorted in daytime hours, or that you are the only person your gran trusts to take her for a hospital appointment.

But your life is also private and you have ownership over what you choose to share with managers and what you don't, providing your choices don't contravene the law, school policy or government guidance. For example, you may like to party hard on a Friday night. Providing this doesn't impact on your ability to carry out your teaching role and that you don't post pictures of yourself with traffic cones on your head on public social media, there is no need to share what you do in your own time with school staff.

The school governors will have a policy on absence, which should include parental absence and may include reference to non-caring absence, or other reasons for unpaid leave. While your work–life balance is your own, you also need to be aware that the solutions you find for managing your balance can impact on others. School managers need to balance the needs of the many with the needs of the few and there may be times when your solution puts other staff or school systems out of kilter. It is important that your personal needs are taken into account if they affect how you can undertake your professional role, but it is equally important for you to be professional and take responsibility to minimise the impact of personal needs within the workplace. There is a lot to be said for leaving your problems at the door of the school, putting on your professional face and giving your best for the children in your class. Dwelling too much on things that you can't change when you are at work can be detrimental to your teaching, your professional relationships and the children's learning. There will be times when this is not so easy though. Chapter 6 will offer ideas on how to manage anxiety that can arise when you are feeling out of balance.

# So what?

### Have you ever balanced a tower of pebbles on a beach?

Beigi et al (2018) synthesised studies on flexible work arrangements to include the importance of one size not fitting all. However, when the Department for Education launched their *School Workload Reduction Toolkit* in 2018, there were some key areas for school staff to consider in tackling their concerns relating to workload: data management, feedback and marking, curriculum planning and resources, behaviour management, communications, well-being and workload. In other words, the role of the teacher. The toolkit can be interpreted as inadvertently promoting a 'one-size-fits-all' response within individual schools. But there is a fine balance to be achieved in ensuring the leadership team are committed to reducing workload and supporting work–life balance within an infrastructure in which individual staff members feel they have ownership and agency over their work–life decisions. Beigi and Shirmohammadi (2017) noted that where workplace cultures were in favour of encouraging work–family balance, the organisational support was more effective, but they also reviewed the importance of flexibility when it is responsive to employees' preferences. In other words, it is one thing to make sweeping rules about no visible marking in books, but is verbal feedback always the most effective way to develop next steps in learning? It is fine to say no work emails between the hours of 6.00pm and 8.00am, or no one in the school building after 4.30pm on a Friday, but many teachers who are parents like the flexibility of leaving school by 4.00pm to spend time with their own children, bartering an hour or so in the evening for planning, once the children have gone to bed. This may be just the time that colleague teachers have agreed is not a good time to email. 'Agreed' is the key word here. Are you confident that these rules benefit staff and children or are they nothing more than a performative measure for a leadership team who are 'tackling workload' on behalf of their team?

Emotional capital and agency are key themes in this book and it is important to consider when agreements are shared or when they are reluctant on your part (or that of your colleagues'). Clark's (2000) research on work/family border theory recognised that, for some, flexible boundaries in the workplace just added pressure on the employee. For example, a headteacher may appear to offer flexibility by requiring a part-time teacher to work on a day that they are not normally required to work, for example an inset day. The headteacher may even offer the teacher pay for the day, where this is an additional day to their contracted hours. But later in the term, the headteacher is not flexible when the teacher needs to swap days for a sudden family-related issue. The teacher has little power to argue their case and has to just chip off a little goodwill. Clearer borders between work and home may have helped this teacher, if they didn't otherwise have any agency. Clarifying these borders can be supported by teacher unions, who are keen for schools to publish their directed time calendars, for example, so that there are not sudden requirements to undertake directed time tasks.

## Have you ever balanced a spinning gyroscope on a piece of string?

Clark's work on the border crossing that takes place between work and non-work is a useful concept for you to consider next. Clark looked at how researchers traditionally viewed work and family as two separate entities, but her work looked at the interconnectedness between these 'worlds' and how the relationship between them was not emotional but, in her words, human. She proposed that people are border crossers and can manage this interplay between two differing spheres, in spite of their social and temporal separation. Figure 5.1 is an interpretation of Clark's work in relation to teaching. Her conceptualisation of border crossing gives a framework to better understand work creep as a border permeation which can be hard to resist. Where the border is flexible, you may see expansion or contraction of one border within another. Work creep is when it is much easier to expand your work border into your leisure area than the other way around.

The global COVID-19 pandemic has meant that for many people, including teachers, there has been an increase in border permeability, as more work has had to be done from home, and those with families have had to manage the care and development of their child while trying to work.

Clark defined balance as '*satisfaction and good functioning at work and at home, with minimum of role conflict*' (2000, p 751). Examples of positive permeability might be where you socialise with work colleagues as friends, or where you bring in a painting you have done in your leisure time as a stimulus for a poetry lesson. According to Clark, negative permeability is often psychological permeability; that is, that the task or relationship impacts adversely on how you feel or your levels of anxiety and stress. This might be where you are asked to complete assessment data in a short timescale and don't feel able to negotiate timings and have to miss a planned event for the evening. This will happen more frequently where you feel there is an imbalance of emotional capital. Having agency will allow you to make better choices about border crossing.

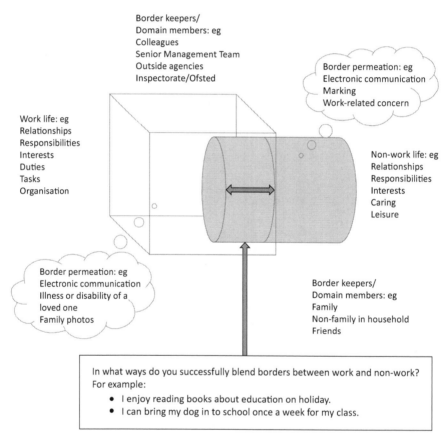

Border keepers/
Domain members: eg
Colleagues
Senior Management Team
Outside agencies
Inspectorate/Ofsted

Border permeation: eg
Electronic communication
Marking
Work-related concern

Work life: eg
Relationships
Responsibilities
Interests
Duties
Tasks
Organisation

Non-work life: eg
Relationships
Responsibilities
Interests
Caring
Leisure

Border permeation: eg
Electronic communication
Illness or disability of a
loved one
Family photos

Border keepers/
Domain members: eg
Family
Non-family in household
Friends

In what ways do you successfully blend borders between work and non-work?
For example:
- I enjoy reading books about education on holiday.
- I can bring my dog in to school once a week for my class.

**Figure 5.1 Border crossing**

Clark proposed that

> '*border crossers who are central participants in a domain (i.e. who have identification and influence) will have more control over the borders of that*

*domain than those who are peripheral participants'*. In addition, those who are central participants in both domains will have greater work–life balance

(Clark, 2000, p 761)

## Reflective task ◀◀◀

- Reflect on your own domains and borders and complete the following chart.

- If you are able to discuss with a colleague or mentor as you complete it, talk about the differences and similarities in your permeations and priorities.

- Use the examples where you blend successfully and think about why that might be.

- Can you apply this learning to help you better manage some of your more negative permeations?

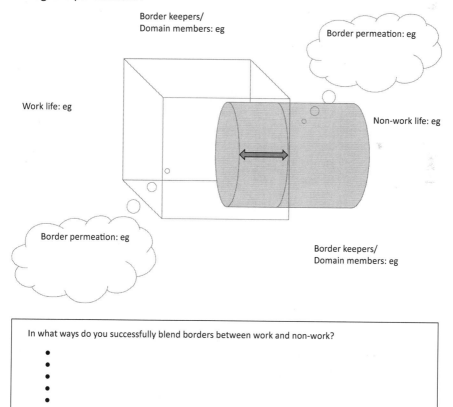

In what ways do you successfully blend borders between work and non-work?

- •
- •
- •
- •
- •

**Figure 5.2 Border crossing template**

Later in this chapter, we look at additional strategies to achieve better balance.

# Case study ◄◄◄

## Have you ever balanced on a tower of stacked milk crates?

Kris is in her early thirties and is a postgraduate teacher trainee. She has two children: one is now twelve and the other is two. She lives close to her mother and currently has no partner.

*I have worked so hard to get here. I dropped out of university the first time, as I had my daughter. I could have stayed, but it was all a bit much really. My mum was a fantastic support and my dad helped out too, although he lives in France. It took me a while to realise that I could be a good mum and have a career, even though everyone had been telling me this from the start. I needed to stop using my unintended motherhood as an excuse. I got a job in the local school as a teaching assistant and really enjoyed it. People told me I was good at it and the children I worked with made real progress. With some guidance I found a part-time degree course in Teaching and Learning Support, which I thought would be a good stepping stone. It meant I could carry on working and mum looked after Em while I did my evening classes and some study time. The rest of the time I had to eke out by getting up early in the morning and reading late at night after Em had gone to bed. It took me three years but I got there and then I started a serious relationship and before I knew it we had moved in together. My partner had a really well-paid job, so there was no rush to improve my career and I was enjoying life. We could afford to go out to eat and we both loved clubs and music venues. It felt like I'd missed all that out by having to be sensible for so long. Looking back, I know my mum was worried but she didn't say anything, but eventually my dad called me and said he felt I'd forgotten my priorities. You can imagine how that went down. I didn't speak to either of them for a month or so and then it was only to tell them that Jak and I had decided to have a baby. We did. It was all fine, mum and dad seemed okay eventually and we were all getting on again and life seemed good. Then as suddenly as it started, my relationship finished and I was left with two children, drastic reduction in income, no social life and few prospects. Dad was in the UK for a while and he and mum took me out and asked me what I wanted most. I knew I had to make some better decisions. My children are my world, but I felt like I shouldn't have to choose between one thing or the other. I just needed to find a way to balance it all. I told my parents I wanted to finish what I had started and become a teacher. I was lucky that they were able to give me some financial support.*

*Teacher training is a really hard year. I can't juggle my hours like I did with my degree; it's full on. I guess it's good practice for when I'm teaching, but I do still want to run away sometimes. My friends help with my occasional crises and bring me tissues and flowers when I'm crying down the phone, or threatening to pack it all in. They have been amazing. I've been treating myself to a club night once a month, during the autumn term, which does me good and I try to do some yoga at least twice a week. Sometimes Em and Vee join in, which sounds more fun than it actually is.*

*I know I need to concentrate on my teaching placements now, but I don't want to give up all my life. I feel like I can only do what I do now because of the kindness of those around me, but I should be able to do it for myself. That can be frustrating, feeling like an adult/child, in debt to my parents, but not sure I have a choice until I can draw down a decent salary. I just hope I'm in a position to look after them if they need it – just not too soon! I've made a plan of the next six months, which is like a giant patchwork made up of small hexagons, one for each day. I've got a colour system going and if I feel a day is mostly a work day I colour it in green; if it's been mostly a family-centred day then I colour it in red; and if it has mostly been a 'self-indulgent' day, I colour it in purple. If I have overall enjoyed the day I put a smiley face on the top, but don't put any negative emojis if the day hasn't been so great, so I don't dwell on the negative. It's a good way for me to stay focused on my priorities, but also feel like I'm all of me too.*

# Now what? ◄ ◄ ◄

## Have you ever balanced a spinning beachball on your finger?

You have been focusing on getting your balance right during term time, but what about the holidays? You are probably already tired with everyone assuming you can just relax for 13 weeks of the year, but you haven't even begun to tackle your own holiday guilt. After spending the first week and a half of the summer holiday clearing out your old classroom, moving into your new one and helping a few colleagues on the way, you find yourself, in the second half of the summer holiday, with the Jiminy Cricket of teacher tasks whispering in your ear: *'You haven't updated your curriculum plan yet, have you? Have you done all those health and safety online learning modules? You know you have to read* Keeping Children Safe in Education *before September, don't you? Didn't you promise to read that book on cyber bullying?'*, and so it goes on. If you're lucky, you can ignore that small voice for so long and distract yourself with sun, sea and sangria, but for most teachers holiday guilt is a real thing. It is important to tackle it so that work creep doesn't infect time that is vital for re-energising and well-being. You are entitled to your holidays; they are part of your teacher terms and conditions so if you choose to do some work, that should be because it is your choice and not because you feel obliged. It is a really important time to make decisions about your professionally acceptable workload. When you are confronted with a nagging thought about a work task in the holidays, test the necessity of the timing with these few questions.

» Will doing this task right now make a positive difference to the quality of learning in my class and to the outcomes for the children?

» Does this task improve my professional knowledge and build my own capital?

» Will I be able to find time to do this task once term has started?

» Do I enjoy doing this task?

» Will this impact adversely on my personal relationships if I do this now?

» Is this task a priority for today? If so, why?

Work relating to teaching and education can be hugely pleasurable and rewarding. If you choose to work because you can answer the questions above in favour of doing the task outside of term time, don't be shamed into *not* doing work either, by friends and family who have an opinion on how you should spend your holiday time. It's your life in balance; your choices; your responsibility.

## Practical task for tomorrow ◀◀◀

### Have you ever balanced an apple on a pear?

You have considered lives in balance and some of the strain of not getting this right at times. Feeling you have agency in decisions about your work–life balance is important and you will recall that if you are feeling motivated and positive this helps agency and agency helps a feeling of positivity.

Don't spend too long on this task; it just helps to remind you of the wider benefits of your teaching career.

• You've already looked at the ways you can successfully blend work and non-work, but build on this and focus on the aspects of your role which further enrich your home life and make a list of them. For example, you might have been teaching French to a Year 5 class at primary school and then decided to take up a French class. You may be teaching Roman history next term and so book yourself a weekend in Rome. Anything is possible.

- You can decorate the list if you wish, or type it up and frame it, but at the very least it is probably worth sticking it on the wall or the fridge to pick you up when your balance is feeling a little wobbly.

## Practical task for next week ◀◀◀

### Have you ever managed a yoga side plank pose, a vasisthasana?

If you, or someone you know, practises yoga, then you may consider it the art of achieving internal and external balance. A good yoga instructor will not see this as a static goal (which once achieved becomes your go-to pose) but instead will seek to encourage you to refresh how you approach your balance as you reflect the changes in your moods, circumstances and physical fitness. Effective teacher mentoring will do the same, encouraging you to hone, stretch and flex your skills and thinking, as you reflect on what works for you, moment by moment.

- Next week, fill in the 'yoga diary' on the next page. Use the bubbles to reflect on your priorities throughout the week by writing in one word or phrase each day which captures your 'pose' for that day and any explanatory comments you might like to add. Think of how you felt about your work–life balance that day and make up a name, as though it were a yoga position. For example, you have an observation the next day and have stayed late in school the evening before, going over and over your plans, touching up a display and re-marking some books, even though you knew your marking was already effective and your plans thorough. This meant that you missed seeing your sister when she called round to your house for a chat. You might capture this as: *'The reluctant perfectionist – missed my sister'.* The next day, the observation goes well, you get fabulous feedback and treat yourself to a film that evening. You might call this: *'The smash-it!'*

- If you would prefer, you can just write a few keywords to sum up your day rather than a catchy title, but either way, reflect back on these bubbles at the end of your week and consider whether you have had balance overall, or if you need to change something for next week. Things you can do to adjust your balance might include:

  - making time to see your sister;

  - rewarding one evening spent working by deliberately leaving your laptop and mobile phone in another room the following evening;

- turning off the notifications on your work email, so it is your decision if you look at your emails;

- set your alarm half an hour earlier to write two reports each morning for three weeks, leaving your evenings relatively unaffected (remember last year you were a nightmare to live with at reports time!).

Be playful with your solutions. Using creative thought helps to keep you motivated and energised, both of which are important in staying on top of your work–life balance.

**Figure 5.3 Yoga diary**

# Practical task for the long term ◀◀◀

## Have you ever balanced as part of a human chair trick?

The human chair trick is where people form a circle or square of chairs, sit on them and then lay across each other's laps, so that the circle is enclosed with no gaps. Someone outside of the circle then removes the chairs one by one and all the participants remain balanced, seemingly in space, until someone gives way and the human chair trick collapses. A good mentor will be like the invisible chair at times; having given you that support to balance by yourself, your mentor will not be far away if you collapse to the floor (metaphorically, of course!).

Good relationships are vital in achieving a life in balance. Having people in whom you can trust and who put their trust in you is affirming and enables healthy personal and professional development. Having the support of a mentor who understands the importance of a professionally acceptable workload and good balance can make such a difference to you in your early career.

The tedium of repetitive tasks is a constant challenge for teachers, but unlike many jobs the repetitive tasks are relatively small. Each day children bring something different to the lessons you have prepared and ensure a dynamism to the role. However, there will be times when a good mentor needs to remind you of what just has to be done (you know it really) and times when your mentor can be more understanding and engage with you on your barriers to certain tasks and how to overcome them. This form of boundaried flexibility can make all the difference to how your relationship with your mentor develops in your early career. An effective mentor will know how and when to remind you of boundaries in your workload, such as meaningful deadlines and purposeful marking and how and when to encourage you to hold boundaries for yourself. If you have no support for maintaining boundaries in your workload, for example if timescales are constantly flexible, the message you receive is that the tasks are unimportant and your work towards those tasks is not valued or validated. An effective mentor will work with you to ensure you can articulate why a task is important, what difference it can make to outcomes for children and why the timescale helps the task to be more effective. This type of mentoring is a good example of teacher learning as an evolving and enhancing process, or a *pedagogy of becoming*, as outlined in Chapter 3. Building up this understanding will help you to prioritise the repetitive tasks at times when you would rather do something novel and more creative, enabling you to balance the dull with the more delightful aspects of your job.

If you have the opportunity, professional supervision is a great way to have an ongoing conversation about teaching and about you as a teacher. Consultative mentoring will enable you to achieve an effective balance in your life, not least because a great mentor will support you to be fulfilled in your teaching and recognise your successes for yourself, working with you on next steps.

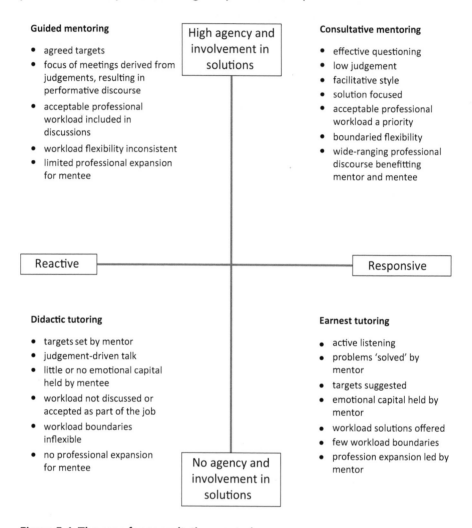

**Guided mentoring**

- agreed targets
- focus of meetings derived from judgements, resulting in performative discourse
- acceptable professional workload included in discussions
- workload flexibility inconsistent
- limited professional expansion for mentee

High agency and involvement in solutions

**Consultative mentoring**

- effective questioning
- low judgement
- facilitative style
- solution focused
- acceptable professional workload a priority
- boundaried flexibility
- wide-ranging professional discourse benefitting mentor and mentee

Reactive — Responsive

**Didactic tutoring**

- targets set by mentor
- judgement-driven talk
- little or no emotional capital held by mentee
- workload not discussed or accepted as part of the job
- workload boundaries inflexible
- no professional expansion for mentee

No agency and involvement in solutions

**Earnest tutoring**

- active listening
- problems 'solved' by mentor
- targets suggested
- emotional capital held by mentor
- workload solutions offered
- few workload boundaries
- profession expansion led by mentor

**Figure 5.4 The case for consultative mentoring**

- Your task for the long term is to find ways to make an equal contribution to your relationship with your mentor or professional supervisor; the more you know about mentoring, the better you will be able to respond and develop as a mentee. And what a great mentor you will be to a colleague in a year or so!

# What next? ◀◀◀

## Have you ever spun a spinning top so that it flipped onto its stem?

Jerrim et al (2020) have examined 11 social studies through three datasets and concluded that teachers are not disproportionately affected by poor mental health and well-being, relative to other occupational groups. The researchers do recognise that this still leaves '*a non-trivial number of school staff facing mental health issues, some of which may be caused or aggravated by their work*' (Jerrim et al, 2020, p 29). One recurring theme in qualitative studies about work–life balance is the perception, and at times the reality, of pressure imposed from senior leaders. It is worth noting here that in a survey of 27,000 randomly sampled workers across Europe (Artz et al, 2020), 'education' came out 17th out of 20 employment sectors, in response to questions ascertaining whether they had a 'bad boss'. Thirteen per cent of Europe's workers report that they have a bad boss, but within education, only 10 per cent. The research shows that in many cases it is lack of skills and technical ability, not malice, that makes workers feel they have a bad boss. In teaching, like many other professions, the workforce requires credibility from senior managers: a shared understanding that the manager, if required, could demonstrate the same standard of task completion (teaching in this instance) that they are asking of the workforce. Yet, if the headteacher or assistant head is really good at their job, sharing a passion to improve children's outcomes, leading with consideration, fairness and a positive drive that brings everyone along, then it becomes less relevant whether they can still stand in front of a class and teach a lesson to the highest standard. Their job is to keep abreast of what the highest standard is and what pedagogy may be best suited to achieving that. Their responsibility is also to understand the conflicts and challenges that can arise from balancing work demands, work-related tasks and a life beyond work.

Your job is to be the best teacher you can be, ensuring you are effective in enabling your pupils to achieve, while developing your skills and strengths. A fulfilling role is often a challenging role and part of that challenge will be to find ways to recalibrate your balance throughout your career.

## Further reading

Black, Asian and Minority Ethnic Educators (BAMEed) network – great resources and connections to multiple and diverse sites and social media. [online] Available at: www.bameednetwork.com (accessed 25 July 2020).

CollectivED – the centre for mentoring, coaching and professional learning. [online] Available at: https://www.leedsbeckett.ac.uk/research/collectived/ (accessed 9 October 2020).

Education Support – tools and resources to support you in considering your working balance. [online] Available at: www.educationsupport.org.uk/grappling-work-life-balance (accessed 24 July 2020).

Joyga – Laura Pintea's blog on the importance of balance poses in yoga. [online] Available at: www.joyga.org/balance-yoga-and-how-balance-poses-can-help-us-in-our-day-to-day-life (accessed 25 July 2020).

Ludus Ludi – balancing games and toys from a company in Spain. [online] Available at: www.ludusludi.com/products (accessed 25 July 2020).

# References

Akobo, L A and Stewart, J (2020) Contextualising Work–life Balance: A Case of Women of African Origin in the UK. *Industrial and Commercial Training*, 52(3). [online] Available at: www.emerald.com/insight/content/doi/10.1108/ICT-09-2019-0092/full/html (accessed 24 July 2020).

Artz, B, Goodall, A J and Oswald, A (2020) How Bad Are Bad Bosses? *Industrial Relations. A Journal of Economy and Society*, 59(1): 3–39. [online] Available at: https://doi.org/10.1111/irel.12247 (accessed 13 July 2020).

Beigi, M and Shirmohammadi, M (2017) Qualitative Research on Work–Family in the Management Field: A Review. *Applied Psychology*, 66(3): 382–433. [online] Available at: https://iaap-journals.onlinelibrary.wiley.com/doi/10.1111/apps.12093 (accessed 28 July 2020).

Beigi, M, Shirmohammadi, M and Stewart, J (2018) Flexible Work Arrangements and Work–Family Conflict: A Metasynthesis of Qualitative Studies Among Academics. *Human Resource Development Review*, 17(3): 314–36. [online] Available at: https://journals.sagepub.com/doi/10.1177/1534484318787628 (accessed 14 September 2020).

Clark, S C (2000) Work/family border theory: A new theory of work/family balance. *Human Relations*, 53(6): 747-770. [online] Available at: https://dx.doi.org/10.1177/0018726700536001 (accessed 14 September 2020).

Department for Education (DfE) (2018) *School Workload Reduction Toolkit*. [online] Available at: www.gov.uk/guidance/school-workload-reduction-toolkit (accessed 28 July 2020).

Foster, D (2019) *Teacher Recruitment and Retention in England*. Briefing Paper Number 7222, 16 December 2019. London: House of Commons Library. [online] Available at: https://researchbriefings.files.parliament.uk/documents/CBP-7222/CBP-7222.pdf (accessed 26 July 2020).

Jerrim, J, Sims, S, Taylor, H and Allen, R (2020) How does the mental health and wellbeing of teachers compare to other professions? Evidence from eleven survey datasets. Review of Education. BERA: Wiley Online library. Available at: https://bera-journals.onlinelibrary.wiley.com/doi/full/10.1002/rev3.3228 (accessed 14 September 2020).

Kalliath, T and Brough, P (2008) Work–life Balance: A Review of the Meaning of the Balance Construct. *Journal of Management & Organization*, 14(3): 323-7. [online] Available at: https://doi.org/10.5172/jmo.837.14.3.323 (accessed 24 July 2020).

Kelliher, C, Richardson, J and Boiarintseva, G (2018) All of Work? All of Life? Reconceptualising Work-life Balance for the 21st Century. *Human Resource Management Journal*, 29(2): 97–112. [online] Available at: https://onlinelibrary.wiley.com/doi/full/10.1111/1748-8583.12215 (accessed 24 July 2020).

Office for National Statistics (ONS) (2020) *Parenting in Lockdown: Coronavirus and the Effects on Work-life Balance*. Newport: ONS. [online] Available at: www.ons.gov.uk/peoplepopulationandcommunity/healthandsocialcare/conditionsanddiseases/articles/parentinginlockdowncoronavirusandtheeffectsonworklifebalance/2020-07-22 (accessed 26 July 2020).

Parratt, C M (1998) Little Means or Time: Working-class Women and Leisure in Late Victorian and Edwardian England. *The International Journal of the History of Sport*, 15(2): 22-53. [online] Available at: www.tandfonline.com/doi/pdf/10.1080/09523369808714027 (accessed 25 July 2020).

Prévost, R, Whiting, E, Lefebvre, S and Sorkine-Horung, O (2013) Make It Stand: Balancing Shapes for 3D Fabrication. *ACM Transactions on Graphics*, 32(4): 1-10. [online] Available at: https://dl.acm.org/doi/abs/10.1145/2461912.2461957 (accessed 24 July 2020).

# Chapter 6    What's over your mountain?

## What? (The big idea)

*Well dammit I didn't get to the top. Now I'm ashamed of myself because now that I know how to come down a mountain I know how to go up and that I can't fall off, but now it's too late.*

(Kerouac, 1958/2000, p 86)

Throughout this book, you have considered ways to achieve a professionally acceptable workload. You have done some soul-searching, aimed to take ownership of the aspects you can control and looked at your responsibilities. The strategies you have been trying are all designed to make a difference, but it may be that your workload is still getting you down. Early findings from the Nuffield Foundation's longitudinal study into the health of teachers in England over the past 25 years has found that one in 20 teachers report a mental health problem that is serious enough to have lasted longer than a year. While that figure is currently in line with other professions, such as nurses, accountants and human resources, it doesn't take away from the difficulties for teachers of managing a mental health need while trying to do your best for the children you teach. The percentage of teachers reporting serious mental health concerns has also risen from only one per cent in the 1990s to the current rate of five per cent.

From a positive perspective, an increase in figures relating to mental health may be the result of campaigns to raise awareness and to speak out about feelings and anxieties. The destigmatising of mental health issues for children, young people and adults in the UK can be attributed to charities such as the Royal Foundation, Mind Cymru, Action for Mental Health and the Scottish Association for Mental Health, to name just a few, who have further influenced policymakers within governments across the four nations. Charities such as Anna Freud National Centre for Children and Families, Place to Be and Young Minds all promote the education of children to recognise the universality of mental health, and resources such as the Mentally Healthy Schools website collate available lesson and intervention resources. Teaching children about mental health can be a good way to think about your own mental health needs too, but supporting the mental health needs of children and their families can also increase your own stress and workload.

Education Support is a charity which specifically supports the well-being of education professionals, but you have to be aware you have a problem in order to address it. Many teachers absorb the burden of workload in the assumption that this is 'just what you have to do'. As part of the Nuffield Foundation's study, Jerrim (2020) analysed the Next Steps cohort, which has tracked a single cohort of young people from Year 9 to their current career points or life choices in their mid-20s. Of the cohort, 290 are now teachers and Jerrim reports these early career teachers have higher levels of satisfaction than their peers in other occupations, but they do work longer hours than equivalent peers within term time. The teachers were the group who were most likely to disagree with the statement, '*Britain is a place where hard work is rewarded*', suggesting that they feel both undervalued and under-appreciated. The teachers within the study make up a small cohort, which only includes early career teachers who fall within the age range of the study, so is not inclusive of all early career teachers, but it does still give some significant insight. The conclusion, that the mismatch between early satisfaction and potential for long-term dissatisfaction may lead to teachers leaving the profession, is in line with Nias' (1997) findings outlined in Chapter 3: that teachers start out with high hopes and aspirations and then leave as they become disillusioned. In his parliamentary briefing paper, Foster (2019, p 13) reported from a survey of former teachers that: '*Workload, government policy and lack of support from leadership were cited as the three main reasons for leaving*', all of which can be inferred from the Next Steps respondents.

Klassen et al (2013, p 1292) looked at what caused pre-service teachers to worry about teaching practice across four countries. In their review, they found that disruptive pupil behaviour was likely to be the most stressful element for trainees, but '*workload during the practicum is also a serious job demand and one of the greatest sources of perceived stress*'.

# So what? ◀ ◀ ◀

## Runout: being far above your last piece of protection on a climb

So, as a teacher, you take on the burden of more work than others and you dampen your frustration in the knowledge you will get more holidays than your friends who are social workers, or nurses. But as you read in Chapter 5, it is not always easy to feel that the holidays are your own. A new term starts and you are already feeling overwhelmed. The first day back and you find yourself having to plan, mark, target and predict, so you blame your workload for making you feel bad. You realise you haven't missed seeing most of your colleagues over the holiday and you're not looking forward to seeing any of the senior management, as they will only want something from you.

It may well be that your school systems do put excessive tasks on you, but for some teachers, anxiety is driving how they are feeling and behaving towards an otherwise acceptable workload.

This chapter includes some exercises which may help you to manage your anxiety better, but you should always seek professional advice if you, or those close to you, are worried that your mental health is having a serious impact on your well-being. This may be a call to Education Support (telephone 08000 562 561), a visit to your GP, or considering a therapeutic intervention. You are important and worth looking after.

As you will have picked up throughout this book, having agency and feeling that you have a say in the decisions that affect you is really important if you want to manage a professionally acceptable workload. Bandura's work on self-efficacy has influenced researchers and educationalists. You can see in the pupils you teach that believing that you will succeed in something puts you in a much better position to achieve it than if you start with the thought that you are likely to fail. It is not always as easy to recognise this in yourself. Klassen et al (2013) draw on the work of Bandura to make the association between self-efficacy and anxiety, which holds consequences for the retention of teachers in the profession. They note that:

> When teachers with high self-efficacy are faced with classroom stress, they direct their efforts at resolving problems, whereas teachers with lower self-efficacy display avoidant behavior. Eventually, teachers with low instructional self-efficacy show lower commitment to teaching.
>
> (Klassen et al, 2013, p 1292)

Anxiety will cripple your self-efficacy and low self-efficacy will add to your anxiety. Breaking that cycle is vital. Bandura (1997, p 241) notes that teachers with low self-efficacy,

> distrust their ability to manage their classrooms; are stressed and angered by students' misbehavior; are pessimistic about students' improvability; take a custodial view of their job; resort to restrictive and punitive modes of discipline; focus more on the subject matter than on students' development; and, if they had to do it all over again, would not choose the teaching profession.

In a similar way to theories of growth mindset, which do not accept a fixed state of being, it is important not to get stuck in feeling that low self-efficacy is part of who you are. There are ways to tackle low self-efficacy, and effective mentorship, focused professional development and self-directed study will improve motivation and that sense of '*can do*'. Teachers benefit from opportunities to develop, reflect and further enhance their skills and professional knowledge. Similar to your goals for children, you will know when you have a handle on a skill or knowledge as you will own your own proficiency. We need to move away from the term mastery and its patriarchal inference and own a new way of describing this; '*owned proficiency*' is what teachers and children demonstrate when they '*can do*'.

If you want to climb a mountain, you wouldn't dream of doing it without training or equipment and while you might be itching to reach those peaks, you would recognise you need to start small and build up to your goals. Yet in teaching, there is often too high, or unrealistic, an expectation placed on early career teachers to be able to feel a sense of success easily in the classroom. A greater emphasis on mentoring and agreed steps towards you owning your proficiency will hopefully be supported by the Department for Education's *Early Career Framework* (DfE, 2019a), introduced into some schools in autumn 2020 and rolled out nationally in autumn 2021. If you are an early career teacher (or a mentor or manager), you now know to question forms of support that are overly performative in approach and you know the importance of having agency within the process, as discussed in Chapters 2 and 4.

## To summit: to reach the top of a mountain

Often anxiety displays as fearfulness, or rather fear of a myriad of '*what ifs*'. For example, you may be anxious about an impending observation or a book scrutiny and consequently you then experience a whole range of performative anxieties: What if the children don't respond to the task? What if I ask too many closed questions? What if my marking is criticised? What if I act immaturely or get argumentative when I get my feedback? This type of anxiety can be experienced by anyone at any time and you may already have found some strategies within the book to better prepare for (or prevent) these instances.

However, your anxieties may be part of longer-term difficulties, such as trauma or adverse childhood experiences. It may be that you feel anxious about other aspects of your life and relationships, or that you often worry about your physical health too. You are not alone. Many people feel like you do and then find ways to make their emotions work for them. For some people, feelings of anxiety will come and go, better at some times than others. Having a few strategies to feel more in control of how you feel will help.

Whether you have some anxiety that is caused by your work-related stress, or whether the stress relating to your work is being triggered by your general anxiety, the following task may help you learn a technique grounded in cognitive behavioural therapy (CBT). Recognising the interplay of emotions, thoughts and behaviours, CBT supports individuals to change their perceptions, enabling subsequent changes in behaviours, thoughts and emotions.

Anxiety can feel like you are ascending a mountain with strange and unknown terrain, not sure if you'll ever reach the top. You can imagine all kinds of boulders and crevasses and sheer drops in your way. One way to tackle these feelings is to imagine what is over the other side of your mountain. Another way is to 'play out the film' or (to continue the metaphor) to walk yourself through the mountain journey, imagining you are filming each step and hazard and overcoming it. Combining both techniques, try the following reflective task. This can just be a mind exercise, but if it helps you can write notes, or even write it as a narrative.

When you are relaxed and still, in a place in which you feel safe and secure, focus on something that has been causing you to worry. For example, you may have been worrying about completing an individual behaviour management plan (IBMP) for a child and having to explain this to a parent, whose own behaviour can appear aggressive at times.

## Reflective task ◀◀◀

Start by imagining what the thing that is worrying you will look like when it is completed, or overcome. This helps you to have a tangible sense of attainment in relation to this worry – that it is *doable*, because you can imagine a world in which it is *done*. So, thinking about meeting with the parent to go through the IBMP, hold in your mind that this is a time-limited task; it will be completed on Thursday and by 4.30pm that Thursday you can imagine that you are still alive, sitting with a cup of tea in your classroom and a self-congratulatory bar of chocolate. You can see in that scene in your mind that you have written the child's plan, talked it through with the SENDCO, tried out at least one of the strategies the day before, which has given you a good example to share with the parent, and you have asked the SENDCO to 'drop in' while you are talking to the parent and agreed a code word if you needed some help. You can even allow yourself to play out that scene, so that when the SENDCO pops in, you just smile and say '*I'll see you before I go home*', as the meeting is going well and you had felt fully prepared for it.

Having played out this scene, imagine what you will feel like when you have completed the task that has been causing you to be anxious. Attributing future positive feelings to the end of the task will help to motivate you and may reduce your anxiety before you begin the more difficult next stage of your film.

You need to hoist your camera high onto your shoulder to undertake this next part. Your brain wants to protect you from negative thoughts, so even though it feels like you have already covered all the possible what ifs of this scene, the likelihood is that each time you have started to worry about what might happen, you have unwittingly distracted yourself from this thought and flitted elsewhere in your mind. This time you have to play out the whole scene, disciplining yourself not to cut away, or leave the internal viewer on a 'cliff-hanger'. You might want to practise on an imaginary mountain first, just to rehearse visualising a journey. Once you feel ready, imagine yourself undertaking the task that you have been avoiding. See yourself sitting at your desk, or in your bed with your laptop on the duvet, writing the plan on the school's planning format. Think about filling in the boxes and pressing send to email the draft to your SENDCO. Now see yourself in the SENDCO office. Imagine the two of you talking it through and see your own face as the SENDCO points out something that doesn't make sense, or that needs to be clearer. Visualise yourself composing your face and taking on board the changes that need to be made. Keep going. Overcome the boulders and the scree and the ice patch. Play through to the end of the scene. It was doable, wasn't it?

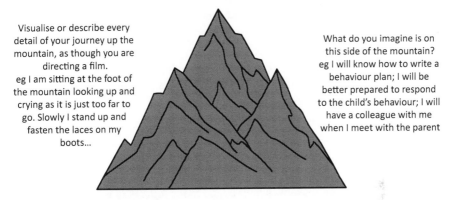

How do you imagine you will feel when you reach the summit?
eg elation, relief, successful

Visualise or describe every detail of your journey up the mountain, as though you are directing a film.
eg I am sitting at the foot of the mountain looking up and crying as it is just too far to go. Slowly I stand up and fasten the laces on my boots...

What do you imagine is on this side of the mountain?
eg I will know how to write a behaviour plan; I will be better prepared to respond to the child's behaviour; I will have a colleague with me when I meet with the parent

**Figure 6.1 The other side of the mountain**

## Back at ground level

The reality may not play out exactly how you imagined it, but by that point you will be doing the task or going through the situation anyway, so either you will feel more in control or it has a time-limited ending and even if it is an unpleasant experience you will reach the end. Most things are not as bad as we had feared them to be prior to doing them and this technique helps you to replace negative possibilities with positive probabilities.

## Case study ◄◄◄

**Fall factor: a formula-derived number which represents the severity of a fall. It is calculated by dividing the length of a fall by the amount of rope in play**

Josh is in his second year of teaching geography at a secondary school.

*I think I just lost sight of what was important. I like to go climbing when I can; to feel free and away from it all. But I started making rash decisions and taking more and more risks. I convinced myself that I was pursuing my sport, being a purist, only going for on sight climbs which were new to me without any preparation, but I was pushing more than my limits. Increasingly I was going alone, competing with myself and not wanting to share what I was doing. In school I was barely concentrating and if the children were getting edgy I would just tell them about a good climb I had done. It didn't help their learning but it kept them quiet. Colleagues knew I wasn't right, but if anyone asked me how I was I would say I was fine. I would add things like 'It's the children I put first; they're what's important in all this'. It wasn't really about the children at all though; it was all about me. I was just biding time until the next time I could head out and come across a crux, a really difficult ascent. It took a fall for me to realise that my climbing had literally become a way to escape what was really bothering me: my anxiety. It was a real thing and had crept up on me. I had been worried I couldn't plan good lessons, even more worried that I wasn't planning good lessons; anxious the children in my class weren't making progress; panicked that I didn't know what good progress looked like any more; overwhelmed by too many reports to write, compounded by not writing any.*

*I realised my keenness to be on a mountain was equal to my reluctance to be in the school. I loved the idea of being a teacher, but I couldn't go on pretending it was alright. I was lucky I could still speak with my mum; she used to be a teacher. I thought she would just tell me to get on with it, like she did in her day, but she listened and asked me what I thought I should do next. That was the best thing she could ask. I think if she had given me solutions I would have found a way to ignore them. I began to see that the way I was feeling was stopping me from developing as a teacher. I was just free-falling off the cliff and in my job and I needed some beta (some insider knowledge) to get back into it. I did see my GP, which was important, but more helpfully I spoke to my year head and asked if I could have a mentor again for a while, like I did when I was an NQT. It was great to have someone to check in with, someone with whom I could try out my ideas for lessons to make sure they would enable the right learning from the children. I began to make a note on my laptop when I felt my panic rising about a task and then I would go back to it the next day and write down the way I was going to tackle it and give myself a fair time to do it in. One week I had 17 sticky notes, so I knew it was getting out of hand again, so I chose not to add any more until I had done this lot first. It's not foolproof and there are days when I feel quite low, but most of the time when I go climbing now, I can enjoy the air and the freedom and then come back with energy to do my job as well. My mentor has helped me to recognise I am a good teacher still and it is worth the time I choose to spend on getting even better at what I do.*

# Now what? ◀◀◀

## No mojo: a slump in which a climber loses confidence in their ability to climb

It is easy when you are anxious to see the world with a negative lens. You're already worried that you are a day later than usual in emailing your planning to your year team colleague and you haven't got any time to do this until you get home this evening. Then you spill your coffee on your shirt, burn your toast and trip over the cat and that's before you set off to work. You feel hot and uncomfortable and if anyone told you that you don't have to go in today, you probably would consider it. But teacher identity is a strong force and most teachers want to do the right thing. Teachers took an average of 4.1 days' absence in the academic year 2018/19 (DfE, 2019b). In the last ten years, just over half of all teachers have taken absence within each year and the average number of sickness days taken for those teachers in 2018/19 was 7.5 days. However, when a teacher is managing high levels of anxiety but is dutiful enough to keep going to school, presenteeism may be a bigger problem than absenteeism.

> Government organisations... have been keen to highlight the business case for improving employee psychological health, emphasising sickness absence, turnover and presenteeism (being at work, but working at less than full capacity) as mechanisms through which it affects firm performance.
>
> (Jones et al, 2016, p 742)

It may not be difficult to think of a day, or more, when you may have felt anxious and gone into school in body, but not in spirit. That is not to advocate taking more time off to manage your anxiety, unless you need to, but to recognise the impact on children's learning and well-being if you don't address your anxiety effectively. Your teacher identity drives you to make a difference. You need to be at peak fitness physically and emotionally to do this day after day.

## Social phobia

One form of anxiety that is experienced by many people in the UK is social phobia, or social anxiety. It's perfectly normal to feel nervous in social situations where you are under the attention of others, even if they are people you know.

But for people with social phobia, these situations can lead to intense anxiety. For a teacher this can be crippling, as so much of the job relies on a performance with a variety of audiences, who demand different things of you: presenting a lesson to your class; discussing a child's progress with a parent at the end of the day; presenting your class books and data to senior managers; or a presentation to governors or colleagues.

People with social anxiety fear they are being judged and worry about being laughed at or humiliated. They feel that how they view themselves within a certain situation, such as eating in front of others, or speaking out in a meeting, is how others view them too. Often social anxiety will ease and even go at some points and then come back and hit you when you least expect it.

There is a lot of information on social phobia, including some information in the Further reading section at the end of the chapter, but there are also strategies you can use and plans you can put in place to ease the impact of social anxiety within your workplace. A teacher experiencing social anxiety would almost certainly find this impacts on their approach to how they view their workload. If you find staff meetings difficult for a while, for example, talk to your mentor or senior manager. Don't say you can't go in, but explain that you find it difficult and would like some help to put a plan in place. Suggest you sit near the door so you can go out if you need a few minutes to manage your breathing. Ask if you can record the meeting so that you can listen to it again later, when you are in a less heightened emotional state. See if you can sneak into the meeting quietly once everyone is in, so that you don't have to do the social chat on the way in, if this causes you concern for a while. In each case, don't get stuck there. Make sure there is room in the plan to build up your resilience; staying a bit longer, making a contribution, bringing in cakes etc. If it becomes overwhelming, it is always important to seek medical or therapeutic support. But if you are aware you are anxious, but these feelings are not impacting too negatively, try some of the following tasks. Remember though, a bit of adrenaline can be a good thing, so don't end up too chilled in the classroom.

## Practical task for tomorrow ◀◀◀

### The credit list

This task is quite a simple one. Find ways to record every 'credit' you have in a day and use other strategies to ignore or pass over the debits. For example, if you are travelling by car, notice all the green lights that you pass. Incidentally, if you stop at a red light, just listen to the radio, or hum a tune, but keep your breathing steady and don't be irritated by it. Notice the green lights though. You could tally on paper when you finish your journey, tap your wrist to make a sensory mark, or find an alternative way that works for you.

Once you are in school, notice every time someone smiles at you, says hello, makes you laugh or notices a positive in you or your work. If a colleague appears to ignore you or speaks to you in an impolite manner, just glide through. Keep your response minimal and polite in return and concentrate on keeping your breathing steady. You could initiate a smile at a colleague yourself, or counter the harsh tone with kindness; that's not cheating, but you don't get to add it to your credit list, even though you might have added to someone else's credit list.

So your day goes on. You can keep it going at home if you wish to, or just keep it to your working day. See if you feel any different about yourself and your role on days you keep a credit list. When you get really good at it, you will just internalise the process, but still be able to recall positive moments in the day.

## Practical task for next week ◀◀◀

**Dyno: a dynamic leap or hold that allows the climber to gain a hold that seems out of reach**

Reavley et al (2019) have produced an evidence-based review of what can be effective in treating anxiety. Among the rich information, it also notes that in four small studies on effective treatments for social anxiety disorder, bibliotherapy was found to be '*more effective than no treatment and may have been as effective as face-to-face therapy*' (p 90). Bibliotherapy is the reading of self-help books, so you are already doing well.

Narrative therapy can be another useful technique, although less well evidenced. Teachers generally love telling stories and in this task for next week you will draw on your narrative skills in a way that may prove of interest as well as having some therapeutic benefits. The Tree of Life, developed by Ncazelo Ncube (REPSSI) and David Denborough of the Dulwich Centre (Denborough 2008) in South Australia, has built on work originated with children who have experienced trauma through the impact of HIV/AIDS in southern Africa. Since that time, the work has continued with community groups of adults and children across the world. You will use the principles today in a way that may prove helpful for you in relation to your workload, but you can also find out more about the methods to support vulnerable children within your setting.

The Tree of Life has four parts which you will need to follow. You can take several days to do this and it would be good if you can encourage a few colleagues to do it at the same time. Ideally, the Tree of Life work would be facilitated, but you can self-direct the process.

Part 1. Draw a tree. Use a piece of A3 paper as you will need to annotate your drawing, but you can use whatever materials you choose and be as creative as you wish. You don't need to be talented at drawing; this is for you. Make sure you draw the ground, roots, a trunk, branches, leaves, flowers and fruit. Remember, this is not a biologically accurate drawing!

- The *ground* is where you are situated right now: Write down the name of your school, your role at school, what activities you enjoy, what part of your profession gives you pleasure.

- The *roots* are your heritage: Make a note of where you trained to teach, when you first knew you wanted to teach, people who have influenced you, the names of your favourite teachers when you were young. These roots have supported your teacher identity.

- The *branches* are your hopes and dreams: Write down your hopes for this year and your aspirations for your career.

- The *leaves* are significant people in your life in relation to your career: Mark down those who support you currently in your teaching, educational influencers that you follow, those who support you outside of school so you can be a good teacher.

- The *fruits* are gifts you have been given: Inside the apples or cherries on your tree, write down the gifts others have given you to get you to where you are now. This might be wisdom, nuggets of advice, financial support to see you through your training, resources that have made a difference to your teaching. Include gifts you have given yourself too. Is agency one of these gifts?

- The *flowers* are gifts you have given others: Caption the flowers with ways you have made a difference to others with your own teaching, wisdom, knowledge and kindness.

Interpret each of these in any way you choose. This is your tree for you to build and grow.

Part 2. Put your tree up on a wall. If others are doing it too, put them together to make a forest. Talk to your tree and talk about your tree. Use the tree to narrate the story of your teaching journey so far.

Part 3. What happens when the storm comes? Think about and discuss with colleagues, if possible, what dangers you may have to face in teaching. What does your storm look like? What can shake your tree? Think about the sort of things that can make you feel unsettled or anxious. What parts of your tree help you to be resilient to these dangers and stand firm?

Part 4. Celebrate. Take pride in your tree and all that it is made of. If you are with others, use specific praise to congratulate each other on the strength of your tree, what you like about the stories the process allows each narrator to tell.

The Tree of Life has been adapted for you. It would be really interesting to share feedback more widely with others and see if this works for you.

## Practical task for the long term ◀◀◀

### Wired: a route that a climber has rehearsed in detail and so ascends easily

Bandura (1997, p 401) noted that a reduction in emotional arousal to perceived threats also increased a sense of self-efficacy with '*corresponding improvements in performance*'. In short, if you have effective strategies to manage your response to the things that have previously caused you to feel anxious, stressed or reactive, then you can feel more in control of your own actions, which improves how you approach your work. Responding is cerebral; reacting is emotional. Responding is professional; reacting is personal. You have a professional obligation to respond to the signals within your teaching environment: the angry behaviour of a child, the blunt comment from a parent, the sudden demand of a senior manager. As you arrive at school in the morning, take a minute to prepare your professional self: hold your head high, loosen your shoulders, drop your hands to the side of your body and turn them palms facing outwards. Now you're in control of yourself and letting everyone know that.

You may not always recognise the physical symptoms of anxiety, which help the body to cope with those increases in perceived threat, such as the child who suddenly shouts and rises quickly from their seat, or the unannounced arrival of the headteacher into your room when you are in the middle of a lesson for which you feel slightly unprepared. Over the next week, try to become more aware of an increased heart rate, or a shortness of breath, for instance, and then put some square breathing into place, or place two fingers from your right hand on your left wrist to measure your pulse. Connecting with your body's core functions of breathing and blood pumping can help you to focus when your mind has been racing or flitting from thought to thought. Square breathing is a simple but effective exercise you can do anywhere. Look for a square or rectangular shape in your current environment: a picture frame, a window frame or a book, for example. Focus on the bottom left-hand corner of the shape. Train your eyes to follow one edge of the rectangle upwards while breathing in to the slow count of five. While following a line along the top of the rectangle for a similar count of five, hold your breath and then slowly breath out as your eyes glide down the right-hand edge of the shape you have chosen. Lastly, hold your breath out (this takes a bit of practice) as you count out five again along the bottom of the shape and then repeat the rhythm at least three times, but as many as you like. You will notice your heart rate slows as your breathing becomes more measured and as you concentrate on your breathing, so your mind loses some of the clutter that is causing you to feel stressed, for a while at least. Once you are in a better position, you can make a less reactive plan to manage the issue that has made you anxious.

# What next?

## Red point: a route which a climber has practised several times before and is then able to lead climb

You probably wouldn't want to carry on climbing if you had sprained your ankle, or suddenly developed a migraine. At least, not without taking some measures to reduce the swelling or ease the pain, while staying alert. Yet teachers frequently try to undertake tasks when they are feeling low, anxious or out of sorts. This is not about giving in, or giving up; it is about knowing yourself better, understanding how your feelings affect how you respond to your workload and doing something about it. In other words, taking measures to reduce your anxiety or your worry. Reading this book to Chapter 6 already shows that you want to make a difference to yourself, as well as the children you teach. Remember that these strategies are for low-level slopes only. If the mountains you need to climb appear Himalayan in comparison, then it is advisable to seek some additional help and support. Trained therapists can guide you through similar and alternative exercises in a way that you can't always manage by yourself. In equally supportive ways, a good mentor can lead you on the crux and let you make your own decisions on a red point route, where you have already gained confidence. You may even become a little addicted to those heady heights and seek a headship in a few years.

## Further reading

Beyond Blue – an Australian website with information and resources to support children, young people and adults 'to achieve their best mental health'. [online] Available at: www.beyondblue.org.au/get-support/staying-well/relaxation-exercises (accessed 12 July 2020).

Education Support – UK charity to support the mental health and well-being of education professionals. [online] Available at: www.educationsupport.org.uk (accessed 14 July 2020).

Mentally Healthy Schools – a range of resources for staff well-being. [online] Available at: www.mentallyhealthyschools.org.uk/resources?SearchTerm=staff+wellbeing (accessed 18 July 2020).

Mind – useful information on anxiety from the charity Mind, for better mental health. [online] Available at: www.mind.org.uk/information-support/types-of-mental-health-problems/anxiety-and-panic-attacks/about-anxiety (accessed 17 July 2020).

Next Steps – the website relating the Next Steps study of 16,000 young people born in 1989/90 across England. [online] Available at: https://nextstepsstudy.org.uk (accessed 17 July 2020).

NHS information on social phobia. [online] Available at: www.nhs.uk/conditions/social-anxiety (accessed 18 July 2020).

Price, S (2019) *Essential Guides for Early Career Teachers: Mental Well-being and Self-care*. St Albans: Critical Publishing.

Scottish Association for Mental Health – online training for teachers. [online] Available at: www.samh.org.uk/about-mental-health/elearning-for-teachers (accessed 18 July 2020).

The Tree of Life – to read more about the Tree of Life and its use as a therapeutic tool, see: https://dulwichcentre.com.au/the-tree-of-life (accessed 18 July 2020).

# References

Bandura, A (1997) *Self-efficacy: The Exercise of Control*. New York: Worth Publishers.

Denborough, D (2008) *Collective Narrative Practice: Responding to Individuals, Groups, and Communities Who Have Experienced Trauma*. Adelaide: Dulwich Centre Publications.

Department for Education (DfE) (2019a) *Early Career Framework*. [online] Available at: www.gov.uk/government/publications/early-career-framework (accessed 18 July 2020).

Department for Education (DfE) (2019b) *School Workforce in England: November 2019*. National Statistics. [online] Available at: www.gov.uk/government/statistics/school-workforce-in-england-november-2019 (accessed 19 July 2020).

Foster, D (2019) *Teacher Recruitment and Retention in England*. Briefing Paper Number 7222, 16 December 2019. London: House of Commons Library. [online] Available at: https://researchbriefings.files.parliament.uk/documents/CBP-7222/CBP-7222.pdf (accessed 14 September 2020).

Jerrim, J (2020) How Is Life as a Recently Qualified Teacher? New Evidence from a Longitudinal Cohort Study in England. *British Journal of Educational Studies*. [online] Available at: www.tandfonline.com/doi/full/10.1080/00071005.2020.1726872 (accessed 15 July 2020).

Jones, M K, Latreille, P L and Sloane, P J (2016) Job Anxiety, Work Related Psychological Illness and Workplace Performance. *British Journal of Industrial Relations*, 54(4): 742–67. [online] Available at: https://onlinelibrary.wiley.com/doi/abs/10.1111/bjir.12159 (accessed 14 July 2020).

Kerouac, J (1958/2000) *The Dharma Bums*. London: Penguin Classics.

Klassen, R, Wilson, E, Siu, A F Y, Hannok, W, Wong, M W, Wongsri, N, Sonthisap, P, Pibulchol, C, Buranachaitavee, Y and Jansem, Y (2013) Preservice Teachers' Work Stress, Self-efficacy, and Occupational Commitment in Four Countries. *European Journal of Psychology of Education*, 28: 1289–1309. [online] Available at: https://link.springer.com/article/10.1007/s10212-012-0166-x (accessed 12 July 2020).

Nias, J (1997) Would Schools Improve if Teachers Cared Less? *Education*, 25(3): 3–13. [online] Available at www.tandfonline.com/doi/abs/10.1080/03004279785200291 (accessed 24 June 2020).

Reavley, N J, Jorm, A F, Wright, J, Morgan, A J, Bassilios, B, Hopwood, M, Allen, N B and Purcell, R (2019) *A Guide to What Works for Anxiety* (3rd ed). Melbourne: Beyond Blue. [online] Available at: https://resources.beyondblue.org.au/prism/file?token=BL/0762 (accessed 13 July 2020).

# Acronym buster

| Acronym | What does it stand for? | Notes/links |
|---|---|---|
| BAMEed | Black, Asian and Minority Ethnic Educators | www.bameednetwork.com/ |
| CAMHS | Child and Adolescent Mental Health Service | |
| CBT | Cognitive behavioural therapy | |
| DfE | Department for Education | |
| ECF | Early Career Framework | |
| EHCP | Education, health and care plan | |
| FTE | Full-time equivalent contracted teaching hours | Written as a decimal of ten sessions, eg 0.4 = two days |
| GP | General practitioner | |
| IBMP | Individual behaviour management plan | |
| INSET | In-service training day | |
| NASBTT | National Association for School-Based Teacher Trainers | |
| OECD | Organisation for Economic Co-operation and Development | |
| REPSSI | Regional Psychosocial Support Initiative | Organisation to provide psychosocial services to children and young people in East and Southern Africa |
| SEND | Special educational needs and disabilities | |
| SENDCO | Special Educational Needs and Disabilities Co-ordinator | |
| SLT | Senior Leadership Team | Sometimes called a Senior Management Team (SMT) |
| TALIS | Teaching and Learning International Survey | |

# Index